ALL GOD'S CRITTERS GOT A PLACE IN THE CHOIR

ALL GOD'S CRITTERS GOT A PLACE IN THE CHOIR

Ulrich, Laurel.
ALL GOD'S CRITTERS GOT A PLACE IN THE CHOIR
by Laurel Thatcher Ulrich and Emma Lou Thayne.
    p.   cm.
ISBN 1-56236-226-7 : $14.95
1. Mormon Women—Religious life. I. Thayne, Emma Lou.
II. Title.
BX8641.U97   1995
248.8'43--dc20   94-48846
                    CIP

f   e   d   c   b   a

Printed in the United States

ALL GOD'S CRITTERS GOT A PLACE IN THE CHOIR

Laurel Thatcher Ulrich • Emma Lou Thayne

ASPEN BOOKS

Salt Lake City, Utah

DEDICATION

In appreciation to our common teacher,
Lowell Bennion, and to those who, like him, would
"do justly, love mercy, and walk humbly before the Lord."
(Micah 6:8)

CONTENTS

PROGENITORS AND PANCAKES

𝓑ORDERS AND 𝓑RIDGES

PREFACE

IN 1992 A LATTER-DAY SAINT woman from New Hampshire, Laurel Thatcher Ulrich, won the Pulitzer Prize and—even more prestigious for a historian—the Bancroft Prize for *A Midwife's Tale: The Life of Martha Ballard*. A mother of five, raised in Idaho, a lifelong Church member whose list of church callings indicates a little of everything and whatever is asked, she shares a common branch of belief and service with her sisters in the gospel. For nearly fifteen years, she and Utah poet-essayist Emma Lou Thayne have written columns on their shared perspective as Latter-day Saints for *Exponent II*, a Boston-based quarterly newspaper. *Exponent II* was inspired by the nineteenth-century LDS *Woman's Exponent* (1872–1914), forerunner to the *Relief Society Magazine* (1914–1970). Laurel was to represent the east perch, Emma Lou the west, in geography if not in their flight patterns and opinions.

Emma Lou Thayne is a nationally recognized writer, listed in both *A Directory of American Poets* and *Contemporary Authors*. She served on the Young Women MIA General Board for six years, and from 1977 to 1994 she was the lone woman on the board of directors of the *Deseret News*. As such, she was a well-informed and loving voice for staff and readers as well as management and board. Mother of five, grandmother of eighteen, Emma Lou brings disarming honesty, humor, and creative tranquility to all her undertakings.

This volume, initiated by the BYU Women's Research Institute, offers a sampling of *Exponent II* columns as well as personal essays, addresses, and poetry published in *The Improvement Era, Ensign, BYU Studies*, and *network* magazine, to mention only a few. The authors explore topics of interest to Mormon women: from giving birth to facing death; from poignant and improbable visiting teaching experiences to pursuing genealogy through family recipe files; from the how-tos of sustaining leaders to the whys of listening to teenagers and the wherefores of being good neighbors. These are real women leading real lives in a very real world. They talk loving sense to women and men everywhere.

Dawn Hall Anderson
Women's Research Institute
Brigham Young University

Emma Lou Thayne

ON A COMMON BRANCH

IN THE SUMMER OF 1983, I was finishing a writing project at the farm of friends in New Hampshire, away from the busyness of home. I had known and admired Laurel—almost entirely through her writing—as an amazing Church worker, wife, mother, and professor of history at the University of New Hampshire in Durham. So wanting to know her better, I called to arrange our going to lunch. The rest is in the poem.

She had seemed to me one of those
who makes goodness look easy,
had a following for the reason
that she did not seek it,
had given up all the right things
like sleep and Thoreau's
"enterprises that require new clothes,"
had held onto what turned out better,
like husband and children, history
and the humanity along the banks of its rivers.

In her abundant findings she stitched pieces together,
cared about kith and kin, insufficiencies
and little old sisters—who wasn't her sister?
Homemade data
held up as evidence
of life lived well
and in purity under pressure.

From Salt Lake I liked her on paper,
the almost only acquaintance we had,
side-by-side columnists and
her the gentle reviewer
of my first novel.

I had long since learned how ships sailing
toward the same port forget their points
of departure. But still how could I guess
the intensity of arrival,
the commonality of purpose and joy?

In Durham for a day
I'd called Laurel for lunch.
We drove in her antiquated Olds
to eat sea food, sat across a plastic cloth,
smelled batter in oil, and I was shaped
to a new agreement:

Above that red candle: the bonding of women
like birds on a common branch who bear themselves
lightly enough to stay, knowing the option
of flight, the distance down, the safety
of balance, the need for the other's weight.

Of course there was no end to the talk,
only beginning: The critical tracings of maps
full of expected surprise, two women
with women's lives to account for.

Time and again over years I've seen it
given the chance, the time: with women in Cambridge,
Provo, Miami, St. Paul, Kearns, Siberia, Bucharest,
Brazil, Blackfoot, Idaho, Oakland, Salt Lake City,
Honolulu, Acapulco, women, wives or not,
somebody's mothers, daughters, sisters, friends
all of no age, coming together saying Who are you?
Answering, I know, I know.

They need no one orthodoxy about how to be,
only the willingness to say
Here I am. Intercept me. Carry with me
our women's cargo of salt and honey. Together
in tomorrow's daylight we can manage
an onrushing world. We fit.
With Laurel the day was like

the streams beside our houses,
continents running together in a forest of ideas and birds.
God's hand handing.

All a bright yellow ripple
on whatever I will kneel down for tomorrow.

DIALOGUE BY FAX:

SINGING OUT LOUD ON THE TELEPHONE WIRE

Durham, New Hampshire
Monday, 7 A.M.

Good morning Emma Lou. I want to tell you about an idea I have for our book. Last September, during a family outing in Vermont, Gael and I took our three-year-old grandson, Griffin, to a storytelling festival. There we learned a song that keeps coming back to me at odd moments. This morning, half awake, I thought of it again. The words fell into place as I slid out of bed and into my bathrobe.

> *All God's critters got a place in the choir—*
> *Some sing low, some sing higher,*
> *Some sing out loud on the telephone wire,*
> *And some just clap their hands,*
> *Or paws*
> *Or anything they got.*

By the time I reached the bathroom, I was miming the chorus, warmed by the memory of little Griffin leaning over the pew in the old white church to humpf like a hippopotamus and moo like a cow.

That's it, I thought. That's Emma Lou and me singing out loud on the telephone wire: *All God's critters got a place in the choir.* (Later I found the song in a book.[1])

It was 5 A.M., too early for a phone call to Utah, but not too early to turn on my Applewriter and capture the image. The metaphor is yours, really. In your poem about our meeting in New Hampshire, you called us "two birds on a common branch." Now, with two time zones and 2500 miles between us, we can sing together on the telephone wire. By the time you are up and eating your breakfast, these words will be spilling out of Mel's Fax machine. What shall we sing today?

At the Cabin! (15 minutes from home)
Tuesday, 6:20 A.M.
　　Dear Laurel,
　　I carried your Fax to the cabin wishing I knew the tune to "All God's Critters Got a Place in the Choir." And I wish you could see this Utah canyon I've loved forever. I can never decide if I like it better overflowing or quiet. Thank goodness for both. This was our last sleeping at the cabin, with squirrels and birds in the pine tree outside the long window, cheeping and singing on the morning. No phone to startle us awake.
　　Has fall found New Hampshire yet? Our mountains are maple red and aspen yellow. The whole crew who are in town came last Saturday—only twelve of us this year, with three out of our five families living away and wishing they were here for this half-sad time when we batten down for winter. Last year we had snow to the eaves before winter finished with us.
　　This year I'll likely miss the first snow when I'm in California in early November for the new baby. Dinny and Mike's 4th. That's eighteen grandchildren in our choir. I expect I'll need grandma wings to corral the youngest choir member, Anthony. At sixteen months, he has the attention span of a mosquito and the reach of an orangutan. But he wins us over with his grin and "scuse me" as he bumps from one mischief to another. It's good we had our children as young mothers when we could bounce back from anything. In that long ago time tired was just part of the game.
　　Then I thought the empty nest years would quiet time into a shape I could get my arms around. Do you ever have a day that's long enough?
　　Good morning, Laurel. How does *your* garden grow today?

Durham, New Hampshire
Tuesday, 4 P.M.
　　Gael's garden froze last night. Today the sky is Utah blue, our trees burning with New Hampshire autumn. Sunday some-

one stood in testimony meeting and said she hated October. Hate October! How could anyone not wake happy in such color?

I love October, always have. I cherish autumn leaves and the last of apples, Cortlands white and tart, cracking with each bite, Northern Spys rich and mellow baked with raisins in the microwave. But I think I know what the sister meant. Autumn, like middle age, is a time of harvest, and with the harvest comes the knowledge of winter. The new babies fill other bodies, the time to read comes with reduced energy, the mellowing of temperament with a recognition of how little can be changed.

Still, I savor the sky and the trees and good digestion. I'm making Grandmother Siddoway's piccallili from the green tomatoes Gael rescued from the frost. Yesterday I sliced the last red tomato with the knife you bought at Emery Farm this summer when you visited Durham. The farm stand is ringed in pumpkins now and hardy mums, the Great Bay opening blue and cold beyond it. The impatiens outside my window, pink yesterday, hang in limp green coils today.

Three weeks ago, when Gael and I took our last baby to college, I thought of a poem by Anne Bradstreet written at least three hundred years ago:

> I had eight birds hatcht in one nest,
> Four Cocks there were, and Hens the rest,
> I nurst them up with pain and care,
> Nor cost, nor labour did I spare,
> Till at the last they felt their wing,
> Mounted the Trees, and learn'd to sing.

With a slight change of numbers that Puritan mother could be me! I tell Gael that our house is now too big and too small. Too big for a couple of middle-aged professors; too small when five children come home with wives and husbands, children, and best friends. The last time they were all here, a dozen of us crowded around the butcher-block table in the dining room. Griffin and Alena scrambled up and down the ladders to our lofts as we looked for places to spread out mattresses.

Then, just as quickly, they were gone. Today, home alone writing, I think again of Bradstreet's poem:

> Or here or there, they'l take their flight,
> As is ordain'd, so shall they light . . .
> Mean while my dayes in tunes Ile spend,
> Till my weak layes with me shall end,
> In shady woods I'le sit and sing,
> And things that past, to mind I'le bring.

Hickory nuts drop on the roof as I type. Through my woods I hear the chimes in the university clock tower a mile away.

Sun Valley, Idaho—your home state!
Wednesday, 1:30 P.M.

Oh, Laurel, you'd love it here—the counterbalance to the crowded, full, filling days at home. I'm away. I'm alone in Peggy and Parry Thomas' empty condo. Imagine. Just me and my computer. With a sunny morning uninterrupted by phones or places to be or even to plan for. And no one waiting for me! Just the sweet informings of reading and sleep—and outside, the yellow poplars glowing as if lighted internally like a Rembrandt painting. Time here for the Light.

My friend and mentor William Stafford's poem "Report to Someone" starts:

> We think we're all there is, then a big light,
> and a call comes and everyone understands. . .

Can he have died only seven weeks ago? His inscription in the book I read with new meaning—"To Emma Lou and the kingdom we share." What a kingdom! Of words and access to what inspires them.

And in the same sitting, I opened to Doctrine & Covenants 88:11: "And the light which shineth, which giveth you light, is through him who enlighteneth your eyes, which is the same light that quickeneth your understandings."

And now there's time to let it happen. To write. Yes. Quickened indeed. Having the time to pay attention, the

8

quickening as persistent as a grain of sand in the brain. And then the surprise as it comes up on a screen or a page. The outrageous peace of letting it out.

I never know—do you?—what's there till it appears like invisible ink. To explain what's out there. Or, more often, to explain me to myself.

What a forever crazy, lovely disease we have, my friend. With all of our orchards and kitchens and people to love and laugh with, there exists this need to write.

Durham, New Hampshire
Thursday, 9 A.M.

If writing is a disease (a lovely, crazy disease) do we want to be cured? I think of Mormon historian Juanita Brooks who confessed that when she first started writing she hid her typewriter under the ironing whenever the doorbell rang. It has never been easy for a woman to be a writer, but when that woman is descended from Mormon pioneers the tug and pull of the practical world is especially powerful. Few of us are able to claim the Lord's instruction to Emma Smith: "And thy time shall be given to writing, and to learning much." (Doctrine & Covenants 25:8) I know I have often questioned my own passion for writing.

Interesting that you should quote from Doctrine & Covenants 88. I've been reading that section, too. Remember verse 33?

> For what doth it profit a man if a gift is bestowed upon him, and he receive not the gift? Behold, he rejoices not in that which is given unto him, neither rejoices in him who is the giver of the gift.

I am grateful for all my gifts, for the gift of life, the gift of the Gospel, and the gift of words.

Salt Lake City, Utah
Friday, 6 A.M.

Yes, my friend. Gifts and a place in the choir. Mel and I often laugh that in the hereafter I'm requesting to be tall and slim and a diva! Meantime, I like conversing with you this way about whatever moves or amuses, chafes, or captivates us. To examine an idea, to let it find its way, to talk it over with others in the choir—and with the Conductor. I never lose track of the privilege.

You East, me West—fourteen years apart in age, spanning over twenty years our essays here, like most women different, yet alike in family, friends, church jobs, urgencies, concerns, delights.

Let's see what our singing in distant choirs sounds like on a common branch.

Note

[1] "All God's Critters Got a Place in the Choir," Bill Staines, Mineral River Music (BMI), 1978.

$\mathcal{I}$NNER $\mathcal{M}$USIC

The most interesting things are right there in front of us,
hidden because we do not know how to see.

I know this: If I focus, let go, and wait, holiness will visit.

IMPROVE THE SHINING MOMENTS

THOSE OF US WHO grew up singing Mormon hymns know exactly what E. B. White meant when he said, "I arise in the morning torn between a desire to improve the world and a desire to enjoy the world. This makes it hard to plan the day."

The longer I live the more I think we can best improve the world by enjoying the world—and sharing that joy with others. In *Refuge* Terry Tempest Williams provides a compelling description of her own education in the enjoyment of nature. When she was ten, her grandmother took her to the Bear River Migratory Bird Refuge at the northern end of the Great Salt Lake. She recalls that as the group boarded the Audubon Society bus for the trip through the marshes, a gray-haired, ponytailed woman, passing out cards, proclaimed:

"All members are encouraged to take copious notes and keep scrupulous records of birds seen."

"What do *copious* and *scrupulous* mean?" she asked.

"It means pay attention," her grandmother answered.

Within a few minutes someone shouted: "Ibises at two o'clock!" "And there they were," Tempest writes, "dozens of white-faced glossy ibises grazing in the field. Their feathers on first glance were chestnut, but with the slightest turn they flashed irridescences of pink, purple, and green." Her grandmother whispered that ibises were companions of the gods, that "the stride of an ibis was a measurement used in building the great temples of the Nile." By the end of the day, Terry and her grandmother had marked sixty-seven species on their checklist. On the trip home, the little girl fell asleep on her grandmother's lap, dreaming "of water and cattails and all that is hidden."[1]

Terry's grandmother understood that enjoying the world means paying attention to all that is hidden. A number of years ago, I told a friend of mine that I wished I could draw the way she did. "You could do it if you were willing to take the time," she answered. I thought she was being unreasonable. After all, she had a *talent* for drawing and I didn't. As I have thought about it more, I have come to believe that talent is an inner drive that propels a person to take time. People who are experts at something work harder at it than the rest of us because they see (and hear and taste and feel) possibilities the rest of us can't discern—the stairway in the side of a rock, the hat or vest in a yard of cloth, the unfulfilled potential of an organization. People with talent help us see what is hidden.

A number of years ago I volunteered to take part in an archaeological dig at a local museum. I expected to learn about shards of pottery, old coins, and bones. I learned more about dirt. I'll never forget the day the head excavator knelt at the edge of the seemingly sterile square I had been scraping and plopped down the Munsell Soil Color Chart. This little publication lists 216 shades of dirt, each with its own number keyed to hue, value, and chroma. To an experienced eye—an educated eye—the sharp cuts at the edge of a 25-inch excavation pit can be as dramatic in their striations as the layers you see in a cliff cut through for a highway. That dark circular blotch at the bottom of the pit is a post hole. That grayish-red stripe marks the 1670 occupation, the next level the 1720 addition. The evidence was both mundane and magical. Think of it! Archaeologists can read the dirt that dropped from the feet of our ancestors.

My husband, who is a chemical engineer, reads smoke. He reads it in the sky and in his laboratory and in the wispy curls that trail across the frosting of a birthday cake when the last candle is out. Our children got lessons in combustion with their birthday parties. Smoke, he told them, is made of carbon particles as tiny as bacteria, the same particles that when heated to 1000 degrees centigrade create the orange glow of the lighted candle. Slice a cold table knife through a candle flame and the carbon will identify itself in the form of soot. Engineers call that process thermophoresis. A sophisticated version of that soot strengthened the tires that carried you to church on Sunday and colors the ink that appears on this page.

I grew up believing there were marvelous things, unseen worlds "beyond the veil." It took me a long time to recognize that the veil over the earth was often in my own eyes, that as I learned to pay attention I could experience more of the rapture of the world.

Recently, I have been learning to read cloth. I carry a magnifying glass like Sherlock Holmes, looking for bits of the outer shell of flax stems clinging, after 200 years, to the fibers of homespun linen. I had no idea how many shades of white there were—or how many patterns, white on white, in ordinary cloth woven on the four-shaft looms that were common in eighteenth-century New Hampshire. I have tried to photograph some of this cloth but my slides come back looking blank! Yet turning the fabric gently to the light, one catches a kaleidoscope of patterns, many of them recorded in old letters and diaries—"Double Compass," "Rose in the Garden," "Heart's Delight," "Flowers of Eddin Burg," "Snowballs," "Blazing Star," and my favorite, "Orring Peal."

I was talking recently with a weaver who specializes in reproducing old patterns. "Why did they do it?" she asked. "Why so many drafts for such simple objects—ordinary towels and tablecloths. A plain weave would have sufficed. Why all the trouble?" I don't know, but I think it has something to do with the fact that weaving was the culminating event in a tedious, wet, smelly, year-long process of turning flax into cloth. Some of the old fairy tales record the danger and drudgery of the process—lips licked away from moistening thread, thumbs enlarged from the labor of spinning. When New England women like Patience Kirby and her daughter Peace Lawton (great names for weavers, "Peace" and "Patience") wrote down their weaving patterns they triumphed over the dull grid of necessity. They improved the world by enjoying it.

I try to remember that as I struggle with the thumping duties I impose on myself. Look at that daytimer again, I say. Don't miss the ibis at two o'clock.

Note

¹ Terry Tempest Williams, *Refuge: An Unnatural History of Family and Place* (New York; Pantheon Books, 1991), pp. 16-18, 20.

TIME FOR THE INNER MUSIC

SOMETIMES I ACHE FOR a time like we used to have when music came with the sacrament. Not that the sacrament has changed or the passing of it. Only that meditation during meetings is minimal at best and impossible at worst—when the stirrings, gurglings, ins and outs of a congregation beset the few minutes allotted so routinely to rumination in the chapel. I admit that I used to be one of the greatest whisperers when I sat near some of my best pals, my sources of enjoyment and replenishment. But I often long for time to sit quietly and go inside myself.

When I was a young girl, I went early—to Mutual, of all things—so that I could sit alone at the back of the high-ceilinged Tudor chapel of Highland Park Ward and look at the painting of the Sacred Grove above the choir seats or of the Sea of Galilee behind the sacrament table. If my most profound endeavor was praying that Spencer Drake would ask me to the Cadet Hop, I still had a chance to make contact with some essence beyond my own paltry sense of how my prayers worked by my bedside, because being in a sacred place lent substance to my entreating.

Since then I've come more and more to respect what can happen in animated solitude, in or out of church—the private examination of feelings and ideas, the surprise of connections, the awakening to arrivals. Yet wanting to be alone is, I think especially for LDS women, suspect. You have to practice it like a secret vice, making excuses, covering your trail. Have you ever tried telling a friend (sometimes the better the friend, the harder the understanding) that you simply would like to be by yourself for an afternoon? For an hour? To many, nothing can be more threatening.

Yet how else to find what's there? To turn inner noise into inner music?

In writing I have found that I experience four kinds of thinking, each dependent upon how alone I get to be. It has to be the same for the spiritual plumbing of any depths worth exploring. The first level of thinking is available anytime. At this superficial level I write simple things—lists, mostly. I can also write letters, function as keeper of a house, carry on casual conversation. It's where I live most of the time.

At level two I write in my journal, recount events, deal succinctly with experience. I still can manage here, without much aloneness, to put some things down.

Only now and then do I fence off time for level three, where I must be alone long enough to reflect on what I have been about at levels one and two. Here, as a writer, I may turn an experience into a metaphor, a conversation into an epiphany. Maybe full of possibility, but short and certainly not sustained contemplation. Quick and to the point, even at level three.

But once in a wonderful while, I get to occupy level four. Here the connections are made, the matches struck in the dark. Here the Muse, the Holy Ghost, whatever the ages call it, comes to surprise, suggest, inspire. It can come out of the night like a dream or out of the day like the call of a bird on the sky. Here I go beyond simply thinking to communing. I am set adrift among the subtleties and persuasions of what can be tapped only in long and absolute privacy within my own head. And that can happen only if I allow myself the time and space to travel from one level to another.

That is a luxury few Mormons allow themselves, I'm afraid. In conferences across the world, in classes from Mutual to Institute, in the homes of family and friends, I have heard women say that the most precious and least available commodity in their lives is time to themselves. My mother's generation never took it, although routine tasks of earlier days did leave the mind free for rumination. Today a woman is bludgeoned by input—TV, radio, telephone calls, music, people—being accompanied room to room, wall to wall.

My daughters say they have to take time for themselves routinely if they want to keep their spiritual equilibrium. I've always needed it. I can remember years of taking to the car for a drive, if only for fifteen minutes, when we had five children under ten. Or begging off from a night out socially just to lock myself in the bathroom to finish reading a good book. Or wishing myself past the Cheerios and Busy Book during the sacrament to explore ideas for a Mutual lesson. I hungered and thirsted for quiet time—the time I have come to revere more and more as I've found less and less urge to take on the world in grand rounds with casts of thousands.

In the past fourteen years I have done the outlandish: I have actually scheduled time to be by myself, to be away from the frantic and enticing demands of all "to whom my heart responds." Until I was fifty-four I had never been away alone—not for school, not even for a summer job in college. My five published books had been written late at night and in any crevices I could find, mostly in my storage room study among clotheslines and luggage and the always-there, so often intriguing beckonings of a household of eight.

Then I was invited to participate in a poetry workshop in Port Townsend, Washington, for two huge weeks. How even to consider it? How could my family manage without me? Luckily I've been blessed with a husband who has supported me in every way, but my leaving for what seemed such frivolity was a far cry from leaving for a General Board assignment or to speak to a church group across the country where I would be hosted in familiar settings—and be "anxiously engaged in" what was considered "a good cause." Who had ever heard of such a thing as this new invitation? And what would "everyone" think?

My children were grown and on their own and urged me to go as did their dad. So I went, and we all flourished.

Since then I've legislated time away regularly, one day and one evening a week as I used to do in my General Board calling. Because of their generosity, I occasionally have time away in Peggy and Parry Thomas's empty condominium in the off-season at Sun Valley, just me and my computer and a lovely quiet to wake to and walk in. By getting away, not only have I found the unbelievable joy of operating for hours and days at a time at that fourth level, but I've found that those who occupy my thoughts and time at home have found their way just fine without me. And that I am more than ready—and ready with more—to come back to them when my time away is over.

If my husband traveled as part of his profession—or even to fish or hunt—no one would wonder how *I* was faring at home. Luckily, my husband has come to be as self-sufficient around the house as I ever have been and as happy to welcome me back as I am to see him. Nothing has gone into a holding pattern except my capacity to tap those resources I never even knew were there, even in my church activities as I sped about my business of being busy.

True identity is found only in being anonymous, in not being connected to another person, place, or thing. Only by not being identified by connections can we discover who we really are. Only when I am not my home, my husband, my crowd, my children, my car, my job, my church job, or even my past am I really myself.

Anne Morrow Lindbergh says that true identity "is found in creative activity springing from within. It is found, paradoxically, when one loses oneself. . . . Woman can best refind herself by losing herself in some kind of creative activity of her own, . . . Only a refound person can refind a personal relationship."[1] Or, I might add, find reason and enthusiasm for being all that she can be in any other realm.

Note

[1] Anne Morrow Lindbergh, *Gift From the Sea* (New York: Pantheon Books, 1955), p. 69.

ODE TO AUTUMN

WITH EVERY FIBER of my obsessive-compulsive soul, I resist summer. I resent being lifted from my well-defined path and
dropped into the underbrush of June. Some college professors
look forward to a summer of research and recuperation. I look
forward to a season of chaotic domesticity. Summer brings to
the surface my deepest conflicts. All winter I store away housekeeping guilts that pop out of my cupboards in June, forcing
me into a role I do not like but have not yet escaped.
Determined to be Earth Mother, I become a shrew.

Home with no schedule and the children underfoot, I
struggle for definition. I make lists, I call family councils. I
schedule dentist appointments and answer forgotten mail.
Fighting the blossoming anarchy, I try without success to
mobilize my offspring, who, being creatures of nature, only
wish to be left alone.

June passes. Under heavy skies, I pick my way through a
year's accumulation of unsorted drawers toward the decadent
wilderness of July, a morass of watermelon rinds, dropped
bathing suits, sweating toilets, and declining expectations.
August will be more bearable, I think, because, despite the
heat, I can begin my countdown to September. Slowly I begin
to bend with the season. As popsicle sticks accumulate on window sills, I sleep late. I read *Family Circle*. I forget for a day at a
time to look at the calendar, though somewhere inside me a
time bomb is ticking, waiting to explode.

Summer is for children or for childlike spirits who soak up
sun in blissful ignorance of the week after next. I remember the
day I had my hair cut really short for the first time. I must have
been about to enter the sixth grade. I was standing under the
maple tree in our front yard when a neighbor walked by and
complimented me on my hairdo. I cautiously replied that I
liked it well enough for summer but planned to let it grow out

for school. "You'll have to hurry then," she said. "You've only got two weeks." Her words intruded on my paradise.

In summer, mothers and children shout at each other across an unbridgeable chasm of perception. Some days I feel like a backpacker carrying Grim Duty up the Himalayas of my children's timelessness. I see the boys sprawled on the living room floor, their knees and elbows bent at dizzying angles above the glacial moraine of their science fiction novels. Through the fog, I glimpse a summer day when I was about thirteen. My parents were away, and I spent eight hours curled in a raspberry-colored chair with a stack of chocolate-frosted cookies reading a novel which my father, in his role as superintendent of schools, later sent back to the Book of the Month Club as unfit for a high school library.

One of the curses of middle age is becoming one's own parent. I hear myself repeating my mother's words, "The book will be better after the work is done." My children ignore me as I ignored her. And so, I slog through the summer as through a long, hot pregnancy, knowing that in September I will be delivered. On the Wednesday after Labor Day, with the children back in school, I will be reborn a scholar.

NIGHT LIGHT

"The things I steal from night are what I am."
—Theodore Roethke

IT WAS THE PERFECT GIFT—a pen that lights up to write in the dark without disturbing anyone. A pen designed for my "system": thinking hard on something just before sleep, then focusing on it in prayer, and finally letting the night take over. Without fail, morning has brought exactly what I needed to find: clear, insistent ideas, there for me to snatch.

I guess that I learned about it when I was a student. The night before a test, I would go through my notes, skim pages, read outlines and summaries. Sometimes I would jot a few notes, never more than one page, to force myself to condense and focus. Always I could feel myself getting impatient, knowing that no amount of study would do what the night would. After a couple of hours, I'd bow out of a study session and head for bed, concentrating in general on what I needed to remember, yet not narrowed down to any set of facts or specifics. I would be sure not to talk to anyone or indulge in digression: no music, no reading, none of the calls or chats ordinarily a part of my evenings, just the "system," not unlike mental fasting, the spare concentration on allowing it to work and the confidence that it would.

It did. Invariably. In the morning, no matter how little sleep I'd had, I was awakened by new ideas, new arrangements of old ones, supplements to material already there, connections, combinations, directions, explicit outlines, stories new and old. In all, a fashioning of a way to go that I never could have come up with on my own. It was like being unable to think of a name, then just giving up and getting on with things. Then pop! Out of the computer in the least expected moment, the name. I knew that I could not have done it by my own devices, with any amount of thinking or puzzling.

Later, in tests, whole pages would appear in my head. Or in a talk or a lesson or on the page, possibilities would erupt. But nothing like what came in those first moments between being awake and yet not awake.

The process stays the same. I go to bed thinking about the talk that I have to give in the morning (or a lesson or an article or even a poem or an idea that has cast about for days trying to find its way or a problem pestering for solution). What happens is not worry. It's just the opposite. Worry suggests anxiety, maybe anxiety over inability to find answers. This is far from that. The feeling is almost elation—certainly expectation because I know what will happen. And because it will, the result will be action, the ability to act.

I have to trust whatever grace it is. And I have to allow time to tap into what that grace suggests. Wake up slowly, I tell myself. Actually, do not wake up at all for a bit. Just lie there holding on to what it is. Do not let it go. Do not open your eyes too quickly. Certainly do not talk. Not now. Reach for a pen and pad. (Now a lighted one!) Get it down. Scribble if you must. But capture it. Respect it. Don't argue with it. Don't try to augment or substitute. Plenty of time for that later. Let it have its way. Recognize the rightness, appreciate what you could never have conjured up fully conscious.

Now put it aside if you must. You can come back to it later. My husband shakes his head. What will I ever do if it fails me? I don't blame him for worrying, but it hasn't so far. Sometimes it works even with a quick nap.

In my studio, I can see photographs of two of my favorite Auguste Rodin sculptures. In "The Poete and the Muse," a young woman listens, serenely beguiled by the whisperings of a lovely informant. "The Thought" reveals the bonneted face of a woman of no age rising from stone with a look of such sublime abstraction that even her beauty is incidental to the intense concentration of the brain behind the beauty.

Often, in looking at them, I remember the originals in Paris. I was stupefied by their power, enlightened by the genius of an artist to see and to make me see. I love what they continue to suggest in my everyday life: that inspiration is possible; nay, *waiting* in some region as mysterious and unreachable to me as Rodin's skills would be, regardless of my will or dedication or yearning.

I may never be a sculptor. But in my own realms of endeavor, with my own limited abilities and training—and ridiculously wide-ranging inclinations—I know this: If I focus, let go, and wait, holiness will visit. The muse will whisper; the thought will arrive.

Mathematicians and physicists talk of it as "harmony," even (and I love this) "elegance"—the useful combinations that come through from the unconscious. Psychologists might call it "creative tranquility." I've heard it spoken of as "the intuitive edge." For me, it is as close as I know how to get to the Holy Ghost.

PATCHWORK

I HAVE BEEN TEAM-TEACHING this semester with a literary scholar who is also an accomplished quilter. Because we are both interested in domestic imagery in women's literature, we assigned students several chapters of *Aunt Jane of Kentucky* by Eliza Calvert Hall (1907), a collection of local color sketches based on the life of a Kentucky quilter. You've probably never heard of Aunt Jane, but if you are a quilter you may have encountered a famous passage from Hall's book in which she composes a sermon based on a patchwork quilt. At first reading it seemed a bit saccharine to me. Yet the more I thought about it, the more intrigued I became. Aunt Jane insisted that the doctrines in a quilt were "a heap plainer 'n they are in the catechism." When she sat and listened to Parson Page preaching about predestination and freewill, she said to herself:

> "Well, I ain't never been through Centre College up at Danville, but if I could jest git up in the pulpit with one of my quilts, I could make it a heap plainer to folks than parson's makin' it with all his big words." You see, you start out with jest so much caliker; you don't go to the store and pick it out and buy it, but the neighbors will give you a piece here and piece there, and you'll have a piece left every time you cut out a dress, and you take jest what happens to come. And that's like predestination. But when it comes to the cuttin' out, why, you're free to choose your own pattern. You can give the same kind o' pieces to two persons, and one'll make a 'nine-patch' and one'll make a 'wild-goose chase,' and there'll be two quilts made out o' the same kind o' pieces, and jest as different as they can be. And that is jest the way with livin'. The Lord sends us the pieces, but we can cut 'em out and put 'em together pretty much to suit ourselves, and there's a heap more in the cuttin' out and the sewin' than there is in the caliker.

When we discussed this passage in class, one student confessed to her own propensity for saving bits of old fabric. She had even been considering making a quilt out of the skirts of her worn-out flannel nightgowns. I laughed with her, recognizing a similar habit in myself. For some unexplained reason I enjoy rescuing things nobody else wants.

At this moment I am sitting on a swivel chair discarded from a University of New Hampshire office, typing at a desk constructed from two damaged file cabinets bought cheap at a discount furniture store, facing an appliqued wall-hanging made by one of my seminary classes from donated scraps. I am wearing a faded pair of jeans handed down by my oldest daughter. Our house has some impressive antiques, most of them salvaged from razed buildings or Boston trash heaps, but it also has more than its share of junk. My husband is three-fifths connoisseur and two-fifths pack rat. I am just as bad. There are two wastebaskets in my study. The one to my left is a weathered maple syrup bucket, the one to my right, a shiny black plastic container that once held joint compound.

My intellectual life, like my house, has been built from "jest what happens to come." We moved to Durham, New Hampshire, in 1970 because of my husband's career, not mine. I began a Ph.D. in history a year or two later not because it fitted some long-term life plan but because it was handy and relatively cheap. (Gael's status as a faculty member gave me half-tuition.) I chose history, even though I had an M.A. in English, because the history department was stronger at the time than the English department, and I thought I would get better training. I chose my field of concentration—early America—for much the same reason, though I must admit that the fit was perfect. I now make my living patching together the fragments of other people's lives.

Not too long ago, while looking for something in an old filing cabinet, I stumbled across the results of a personality test I took almost thirty years ago when I was a student at the University of Utah. Most of the scores were quite predictable, but when I came to "Autonomy," I was stunned. My score was so low as to be almost invisible. This from the Women's Debate Champion of the Western States! I may have been a high-achiever, but I was a wimp at heart. Readers of this essay who have the mistaken impression that I am a totally liberated, self-directed person should know that I have never gone job hunting. When I finished my Ph.D., the Humanities Program at UNH came looking for me: they had a low-paying position recently abandoned by another faculty wife. Four years later when one of my mentors left the university, I took his job, a tenure-track position.

Recently I was describing my career path to another woman historian. "I was lucky," I started to say, summarizing my progress at UNH from faculty wife, to graduate student, to part-time instructor, to tenured professor. Then I paused, knowing she was a feminist and would recognize the self-deprecation. "No, I worked hard," I said. "It wasn't easy." In the abstract my career seems like a small miracle. Following my husband into the hinterland, I found my own way. Yet remembering the details of that journey, I think mostly of the numbing daily struggle to accomplish not just two but sometimes four or five things at once. It took me five years to finish a one-year M.A. and nine years to complete a Ph.D. After eight years on the UNH faculty, I had tenure, but I didn't get a sabbatical for a long time after that because the four years I spent in a "temporary" position don't count. Still, the patching and piecing I have done over the years have not only brought me much happiness, they have enlarged my freedom. There are pieces in my scrap pile that weren't there twenty years ago.

My father used to say, "If you can't do what you like, like what you do." I resist the grin-and-bear-it tone of that saying— making the best of things can sometimes mean making less of oneself as a free agent and child of God. Yet I must admit that I do like what I do, even those parts of it I didn't choose. When I hear a student agonizing over what direction to take, I sometimes say, "Stop looking for the perfect major or the perfect job. Pick something—anything reasonable—and do it with all your heart. The next step will be easier." I think that's good advice, especially for young people who are burdened by too many options, who feel defeated by a cornucopia of possibilities. For myself, I feel more kinship with Aunt Jane. Occasionally someone will ask if I have ever contemplated writing a novel. I haven't. I enjoy struggling with predestined facts, rummaging through my piece bag of historical evidence for the forgotten scraps no one else has noticed. For me, writing fiction, as Robert Frost once said of writing free verse, would be like "playing tennis with the net down." Or in Aunt Jane's parlance, buying one's calico at the store. I am a historian because I like detective work, because I enjoy old things, because I love junk as well as art, because my husband brought me to New Hampshire. Because I am a quilter.

I Am Delighted

I am delighted. My life goes well.

I must say it as clearly as I can
before I'm gone.

So little delight there can seem in the world.

Almost as if it's shameful or naive
to love what is there:

A new collapsible pair of glasses
flat in a one-inch pouch—imagine!

Can be worn inside my bra:

Anywhere the telephone book,
a needle, newsprint—it's Okay.

Touch a key on my new computer,
Clean up window. And tiny icons
on a desktop scoot about for space—
alphabetical!

Take a 4 o'clock walk from Ketchum
past the fields and watch a young mare
and gelding frolicking like kittens,
a nine-year-old biker trying to look nonchalant
as he sails past you
with no hands.

Hear the brook getting in with
the white swans at the black pond.

Feel the sun making its last statement
to the fence posts.

Smell the perfume of the yellow haired
lady strolling with the short man's hand.
Nod as the Land Cruisers give way

to the languid redolence
of manure.

Back, find the word you've hunted for:
forage, jasmine, medallion.

Taste the strawberries on yogurt
at your own sink.

Let the shower have its way with
your hair.

Be tired.

After they have stood and sat and walked
and climbed the stairs, put those legs
to bed.

Talk not at all.

Take as long as you need
to find the fit.

And those eyes, let them close.

See, see, particles of delight
to sleep with
and be delightfully surprised by
tomorrow.

Emma Lou Thayne • 1980

SEEING WITHOUT SEEING

Stories. The lasting connectedness between generations, as sure as genes or upbringing or place. My mother at my bedside twirling the corners of my pillow, home from seeing Helen Keller in the Tabernacle, telling her story. Half a lifetime later, her eight years dead, still with me, me telling the story that had become mine. A new setting, a new reason for the telling. The wind of memory collecting the fragments, instinct and imigination her gifts as well, to let a new story tell now about believing.

WHEN I WAS A LITTLE GIRL, my daddy took me clear to Salt Lake to hear Helen Keller in the Tabernacle. I must have been about eight or nine, and I'd read about Helen Keller in school and my mama had told me her story, and she decided it would be more important for me to go than for her. I remember sitting in the balcony right at the back of that huge domed building that was supposed to have the best acoustics in the world. Helen—everybody called her that—walked in from behind a curtain under the choir seats with her teacher, Annie Sullivan. She talked at the podium—without a microphone in those days—but we could hear perfectly her guttural, slow, heavily pronounced speech as she told all about her life and her beliefs. Her eyes were closed and when it came time for questions from the audience, she put her fingers on her teacher's lips and then repeated for us what the question had been. She answered questions about being deaf and blind and learning to read and to type and, of course, to talk. Hearing that voice making words was like hearing words for the first time, as if language had only come into being—into my being at least— that moment.

Someone asked her, "Do you feel colors?" I'll never forget her answer, the exact sound of it—"Some-times . . . I feel . . . blue." Her voice went up slightly at the end and meant she was smiling. The audience didn't know whether to laugh or to cry. After many questions, she said, "I . . . would like . . . to ask . . . a fa-vor of you." Of course the whole audience was alert. "Is your Mormon prophet here?" she asked. There was a flurry of getting up on the front row, and President Grant walked up the stairs to the stand. She reached out her hand and he took it. All I could think was, Oh, I wish I were taking pictures of that. "I . . . would like . . ." she said, "to hear your organ . . . play . . . your fa-mous song about your pio-neers. I . . . would like . . . to re-mem-ber hear-ing it here," all the time holding the hand he had given to her to shake. I liked them together, very much.

I remember thinking, I am only a little girl, probably others know, but how in the world will she hear the organ? But she turned toward President Grant and he motioned to Alexander Schreiner, the Tabernacle organist, who was sitting near the loft. At the same time President Grant led her up a few steps to the back of the enormous organ—it has five manuals and eight thousand pipes. We were all spellbound. He placed her hand on the grained oak of the console and she stood all alone, facing us in her long black velvet dress with her right arm extended, leaning slightly forward and touching the organ, with her head bowed.

Brother Schreiner played "Come, Come Ye Saints," each verse a different arrangement, the organ pealing and throbbing—the bass pedals like fog horns—as only he could make happen. Helen Keller stood there—hearing through her hand—and sobbing.

Lots of us in the audience were mouthing the words to ourselves: "Gird up your loins, fresh courage take, our God will never us forsake, and then we'll have this tale to tell—all is well, all is well." I could see my great-grandparents, converts from England and Wales and France and Denmark in that circle of their covered wagons, singing over their fires in the cold nights crossing the plains. Three of them had babies die, all under two, and my grandmother Stanton—great grandpa's second wife whom he loved—was buried in Wyoming. "And should we die, before our journey's through, Happy day! All is well. We then are free from toil and sorrow too. With the just we shall dwell. But if our lives are spared again to see the Saints their rest obtain, Oh how we'll make this chorus swell. All is well! All is well!"

So then, that Tabernacle, that singing, my ancestors welling up in me, my daddy beside me, that magnificent woman all combined with the organ and the man who played it and the man who had led her to it, and whatever passed between the organ and her passed on to me. I believed. I believed it all—the seeing without seeing, the hearing without hearing, the going by feel toward something holy, something that could make her cry and could lift my scalp right off, something as unexplainable as a vision or a mystic connection, something entering the pulse of a little girl, something that no matter what, would never go away. What it had to do with Joseph Smith or his vision or his gospel I never would really understand—all I know to this day is that I believe. Whatever it is, I believe in it. I get impatient with people's interpretations of it, with dogma and dictum, but somewhere way inside me and way beyond impatience or indifference there is that insistent, infernal, so help me, sacred singing—All is well, All is well. My own church, inhabited by my own people—and probably my own doctrines—but my lamp, my song—my church. I would be cosmically orphaned without it.

My mother's experience, my story, the linking on either side of the veil to knowing what cannot be seen or heard, only felt and absorbed. The believing that transcends any saying except what a story tells.

*F*RIENDS

AND

*N*EIGHBORS

Even the deprivation of Myrtle's childhood took on
a richness as she talked.

"Without soul, we are inclined to satire instead of
compassion."

NEIGHBORS

MORE THAN TWENTY YEARS ago our family moved into a new neighborhood. We had three, almost four small children, and we had built one wing of the house specifically for my widowed mother. To the west of us lived an older couple who had been the only ones on the street for years. They had cultivated quiet and solitude with the same meticulousness with which they pampered their velvet lawns and immaculate gardens. No one in the surrounding neighborhood knew them very well. They didn't go to the predominant church up the street two blocks, and since they had no children to chase into other people's concepts of them, they remained an aloof mystery to those who had occasion to walk dogs or charities past their door.

All the time that we were building we were aware of their indignation that we were doing so. During our constant visits to the site we saw only fleeting glimpses of them peering from their patio or getting into their car. They never said a single hello and became almost spectres that made our imminent move a touch eerie.

By the time we moved in it was nearly Christmas. Winter followed with all of its contained seclusion. Except for a few fox and geese and snowmen in the front yard, no one desecrated the no-man's-land that now lay between the Hugos' property and ours.

Then spring came. Muddy runoff drained from our unplanted yard onto the pool-table-greens of the Hugos' lawns. We built immediate and thorough sumps under the bulldog eyes of our unconversational neighbors. Soon our children were riding audacious tricycles into the forbidden driveway and chasing balls onto the unfenced premises. The sandpile we put in on the west of our house brought an unqualified demand for a high grapestake fence between it and their patio ten feet away.

By summer, loud parties on that patio reverberated through our bedroom which, unfortunately for us, overlooked it. In the bedroom below ours we often rocked and coddled sleepless children wakened by the noise of the parties next door that had no child-imposed curfews. And so it was with little-quelled irritation that we lay in our bed above that patio that fateful Saturday night in July to overhear the Hugos, this time just the two of them, at 2:00 A.M. coming home from a night out. By then we were certain that they were insensitive carousers whose only standards were horticultural and isolationist. After all, what kind of people could be anti-church, anti-neighbor-hood, anti-children, anti-everything that made sense to us, their now very alien neighbors to the east? And what chance had we ever had to understand any of their doings? We had not had a single real conversation with them.

The dialogue between the two of them boomed into our open windows that July night. She had a very distinctive voice and he was very hard of hearing, so it was not the first time we had been inadvertent eavesdroppers on her directives. "These blasted cats!" she exploded. "Look at them—all over our lounge! People at least have the decency to keep dogs home, but *cats!* They run like tramps and ruin things and nobody takes them seriously!"

We stared at the ceiling, knowing that the "cats" were with-out question the two new kittens that our daughters had been loving for the past week.

"What are they doing out?" I hushed to Mel. "I thought the girls put them in the storage room."

Below us, the one-sided conversation continued. She was saying, "You just take them and get rid of them. Go on. Right now. I'm not going to stand for this."

Unbelieving, we lay openmouthed as we heard the garage door go up, the car start and leave. "They wouldn't! Tell me they wouldn't!" we said to each other. Silence. For seventeen minutes, silence. Then the car back, the door up, the door down. Silence.

"You don't really think . . ."

"No. Nobody would just . . . but what else?" There we lay, steaming, till Sunday morning.

Before leaving for priesthood meeting, Mel blistered over to the Hugos' front door. We had searched everywhere, and there were no kittens. The girls had been up since 7:00, hunting and crying. Mel is a magnanimous man and usually slow to anger, but he came back from the Hugos' with his ears red and his jaw clamped. He had to rush to his meeting, but told me that Mr. Hugo had admitted taking the kittens away and that Mrs. Hugo had been furious. She said they would never tell where they had taken them and that what we *really* deserved was to have the police on our wayward backs.

Eight months expectant and holding the hand of the four-year-old I dragged with me, I went pounding to the Hugos' door to demand they tell us where they had left our kittens. When Mrs. Hugo opened the door, I began with, "Do you have any idea what it means to a little girl to have something happen to her kitten?" I'm sure I was lighted up by the outrage that now moved me past any politeness. But I had no chance to inquire further. Mrs. Hugo moved just far enough forward to open the screen door and screech at me, "You get out of here, you troublemaker! You've been nothing but trouble from the minute you came around here. Now get out!" And she slammed the screen and then the door on my now totally fired indignation.

I stormed home bent on if not revenge at least retribution. The girls were crying, and I was blubbering. Mother met me at our door. "I hear there's a problem," she said with her usual calm.

"A problem!" I whooped, and proceeded to crash through the details of the battle.

She let me huff and fume, even in front of the children as I recall, something she never would have approved under normal circumstances. That was undignified and destructive. But when I was through—a grown thirty-two-year-old woman, ranting that I wanted to call the police myself—she sat me down alongside the children and said very quietly, "Emma Lou, this is a pivotal moment in your life with the people next door. You've moved in here, and you expect to stay. Probably so do they. And they were here first. You've introduced a lot of frustration and bewilderment into their established lives. But I'll bet anything that Mrs. Hugo feels just as terrible as you do right now."

"Oh, sure," I huffed. "She's probably swimming in regret."

"You know, I'm sure she is," Mother said. "And it's up to you to make amends."

"Me!"

"Yes, you and your little girls."

I couldn't believe what I was hearing, not even from Mother. Mother had always had unusual, sometimes bizarre ways of handling life and us, but this was crazy. I wasn't going to crawl penitently to someone who had so thoroughly wronged all of us.

"Oh, yes you will," Mother said, with the quiet firmness that had always marked the finality of a decision. "You will help your girls pick the nicest flowers in the garden (goodness knows we had few enough that first summer) and then they will take them over to Mrs. Hugo—without you. I don't trust you as much as I do them. And they will tell her how sorry they are that their kittens were a nuisance."

"And then what?" I asked, dumbfounded.

"And then—good relations with your neighbors for the rest of your time here."

I still thought it was all backwards, but I did remember a scripture somewhere that said something about letting him who has been offended be the one to apologize for whatever caused the offense. (See Matt. 18:15–20.) At any rate, I sent the children off with their bouquets of pansies and castor beans.

Before they had even made it back to our door, the phone rang. It was Mrs. Hugo, and she was crying. "Oh, Mrs. Thayne," she was saying, "those darling children—and flowers! If you only knew how sorry I am! I've always had a terrible temper, and it's ruined my life. I guess we all say and do things we're horribly sorry for, and we rarely get to say so."

I was crying and sorry, too. Standing there in the kitchen, I heard her saying where they'd dropped the kittens, offering to take us there and help look for them, saying she'd like to put an ad in the paper for the kittens or buy new ones for us, saying how well she remembered how much her daughters loved kittens when they were little, how long ago that had been, how much she missed her family, how far away they were, how much she would like to be friends.

I can never remember feeling more warmth flood between two people. Before Mel came home from his meeting, the Hugos had taken us hunting for the kittens (in vain), and we had invited them for dinner. Mother and Mrs. Hugo had chatted about grandchildren and flower arrangements, and I had noticed how much Mr. Hugo seemed like my dear Uncle Willard.

For the fifteen years that we lived next door, the Hugos were a pleasant and broadening part of our lives. Our children came to know them as givers of candy and interest in any project. And they taught us much. Though we still had many things *not* in common, we came to appreciate their need for privacy, their different kind of conviviality, their sincere adherence to a code unlike ours in minutiae but astoundingly similar in principles.

When Mr. Hugo died, it was Mel that they asked to say a prayer at the funeral that was not in our church. Later it was Mrs. Hugo who brought flowers from her bounteous garden to our door as the moving van came to take her and her loneliness to live with a daughter in Detroit. "Thank you for the flowers over the years," she said.

As we held each other in the first and last hug we were to share, I thought how different that departure would have been if my wise little mother had not sat me down and taught me how to let the Golden Rule be more than mere abstraction on a page.

A Morsel of Bread

I ATE A PICKLED HERRING once when I was visiting teaching. I knew I wouldn't like it when I took it, slithery and shining from the dish, but I was too serious about compassionate service to risk offending Sister Suomi. I smiled, chewed as little as possible and swallowed, thinking all the while of rattlesnake meat. My companion's refusal, although I thought it rather graceful, left me with a dim sense of superiority.

My four years as a visiting teacher in inner-city Boston was my substitute for a foreign mission. I don't know whether the Relief Society president planned it that way, but tracking down obscure apartment buildings on one-way streets in dark corners of the city was as good a way as any to initiate a bright-faced young student wife from the West into the realities of urban life. Fortunately, my first companion had lived in Boston for a year and knew how to cope with the traffic. Together we discovered the wrong side of Beacon Hill, the murkier sections of the Back Bay, and on one memorable day, the squalid elegance of the South End where one of our sisters, retarded from birth, lived in a rooming house among cockroaches that didn't bother to hide during the day.

Before long I, too, was Boston-wise and able to initiate another student wife from Utah. My companions and I were serious about visiting teaching and we thought we understood the gospel. Certainly we brought to these adventures a naive faith that sustained us in what could have been some ugly moments. One afternoon, we were getting out of our car on Ruggles Street just as a physician in our ward who worked at a clinic nearby drove past in his Volkswagen. He zipped by, stopped, then backed up the length of the one-way street.

"What are you two girls doing here?" he asked.

"Visiting teaching," we said, balancing our babies on our hips.

"Visiting teaching!" he gasped. "I wouldn't walk through this neighborhood in the middle of the day with a police escort."

He probably knew what he was talking about. Most of the buildings on this stretch of Ruggles Street stood empty, scarred by graffiti and broken glass, waiting for urban renewal or gentrification. We laughed nervously, remembering the times we had driven there at night to pick up Sister Berry for Relief Society.

After that we avoided Ruggles Street at night, though we did persist in our efforts to activate our Sister Berry, a good-natured blonde with no husband and several children, two of whom were black. I think she liked us, though maybe she was only amused by our innocence. Every visit brought forth a tale of stabbings in the hallway or rats in the walls. One day she told us a faith-promoting story. The week before she had been entirely out of food, had had nothing in the house but half a cup of Minute Rice, when something told her to look under the mattress. Sure enough, there was a ten-dollar bill! The Lord had provided.

Sister Berry had faith, though she certainly wasn't counted among the faithful. For a year or two, she got a lot of attention from our ward. Several of us spent a Saturday there cleaning her house, though I am not sure why. I do remember the sense of righteousness I experienced as I defrosted her refrigerator, thinking all the while of what I could teach her about nutrition and budgeting if I ever got the chance. She was marvelously resistant to Mormon values. One Saturday morning, still in her nightgown, she opened her door to two members of the bishopric, making no effort to disguise the presence of a man in the bed just off the hall.

Eventually the elders quorum found her an apartment in a bland but safe section of the city. Not long after that, she simply disappeared, taking her place on the "skip list" that so frustrated the membership clerk.

Sister Chan's inactivity was of a different sort. She didn't drive, her husband ran a restaurant and worked on Sundays, and she understood so little English that she wouldn't have enjoyed the meetings anyway. She lived as far south as Boston goes, in Dorchester, almost to the Milton line. Once a month without fail, my companion and I dressed our almost identical babies, left our almost identical student apartments, and wound our way through the unfamiliar streets lined with kosher bakeries to Blue Hill Avenue. We would ring her bell, wait for the answering buzzer, then walk up the two flights to her apartment, wondering what culinary adventure awaited us. We didn't come to eat, though she may have thought we did. Month by month she laid before us all the delicacies that once went to husky missionaries in Taiwan—delicate shrimp chips, candied ginger, or flaky Moon Cakes filled with sticky black bean paste.

She always laughed when she opened the door, motioning to a row of slippers lined up neatly against the wall. Taking off our shoes, we quickly used up the five or six sentences we all had in common. From then on, it was smile, nod, and eat. We might just as well have been Elijah coming through the door saying, "Bring me, I pray thee, a morsel of bread in thine hand." (1 Kings 17:11) Like the widow of Zarephath, Sister Chan was blessed with a bottomless barrel and a never empty cruse. One afternoon she motioned us into chairs and disappeared, staying in her kitchen much longer than usual. We bounced our babies, smiled at each other, and looked around the room at the brocaded chair covers and bright paper flowers, listening anxiously to the clatter in the kitchen.

The first course arrived, then the second. There were flat bowls and platters piled with food, fried rice with slivers of salty ham, omelets blossomed with pink shrimp and scallions, benign-looking carrots aflame with ginger, and other mysterious dishes dark with ruffled fungi. I thought I liked Chinese food, and we both liked Sister Chan, but we were totally unprepared to carry on this mysterious conversation. She rushed in and out of the kitchen. We ate and ate until we could eat no more. In one desperate moment, when our hostess was out of the room, my companion dropped half a plate of fried rice into a diaper bag.

As Latter-day Saint women we were well versed in the language of food—a loaf of bread to a new neighbor, fudge and divinity at Christmas, a hearty casserole when a mother and baby come home from the hospital. Sister Chan's food took us into alien lands, astonishing us with a superfluity we could not comprehend. We knew better than to reject her beautiful food, but we did not comprehend the isolation or the pent-up need to serve that brought it forth.

In the spring of 1964, I made my last visit to Sister Chan. Somehow I managed to explain that my husband had finished school and that we were leaving Boston. She took me into a room at the front of the apartment and got her purse out of a drawer. Pressing two bills into my hand, she said, "Here is lucky money."

Back home, I looked at the two ten-dollar bills in dismay, student poverty having given me a distorted sense of the importance of money. I puzzled over the problem all the next morning, going to the phone once or twice to dial her husband's restaurant, then resolving to solve the problem with the least embarrassment for her—and for myself. I put eighteen dollars in an envelope and mailed it to her son with a little note explaining that I was sure his mother had meant to give me two dollars instead of twenty dollars. (My reasoning was impeccable. Because she couldn't speak English, she could easily have mistaken the denominations on the bills!)

I am still ashamed of my stupidity. Several months later, a friend wrote to me from Boston to say that the Chans were offended by my letter, as of course they should have been.

"What is twenty dollars," they had said, "when you might never see someone again?"

I hope if Sister Chan still remembers me she has forgiven my insensitivity and pride. I had tried to live by the visiting teachers' motto—it is more blessed to give than to receive. Looking back, I am astonished at how much I received and how little I was capable of giving.

MYRTLE

"For she hath been a succourer of many, and of myself also."
Romans 16:2

MOVING TO NEW HAMPSHIRE challenged my image of myself as a committed and effective visiting teacher. By then I had ten years experience knocking on strange doors and making friends with unexpected people. I even had the satisfaction of remembering how Helen Low and I had gradually brought Sister Mugica back to church, visiting her casually in the grocery store where she worked until retirement finally allowed her to accept our invitations to Relief Society. I am not sure why things were so much more difficult in New Hampshire. It wasn't the distance we had to travel. I was used to that. Perhaps I was simply trying to do too many things. My family was larger, my other church callings strenuous, and I was beginning a Ph.D. program in history.

I was dismayed one Sunday when, having gone to the bishop's office on an errand, I saw my name on a huge chart listing the visiting teachers in our ward with their assignments. Beside my name, a zealous Relief Society secretary had written, "never goes." That wasn't true. I did go some of the time, but I often forgot to bring my report to the meeting, and, because most phone calls in our ward were long distance, no one could afford to remind me.

For a time, I had done my visiting teaching regularly and on time, though the back streets of New Hampshire mill towns seemed less exotic and more dreary than the slums of Boston. Alice Ayer and I had visited one sister who must have been a victim of agoraphobia, though we didn't know the word. She seldom left her house and then only at night and when her husband was driving. Her house was dank with the smell of stale tobacco, the green glow of the television mocking our cheerful messages. When there was a death in her family—no one close, as I recall—Alice put together a casserole and I made a big chocolate cake in my black enamel roasting pan. Three weeks later when we stopped by, she handed back our pans, mine still unwashed, the blackened crumbs so molded to the surface that at first I thought the enamel had warped and was peeling. I was not so much offended by her inability to muster even the appearance of gratitude as by her total inaccessibility. In her presence, my purposefulness became an embarrassing protuberance, like a wart.

One sister who did even more to temper my idealism was Evelyn Johnson. She was a widow in her early seventies, severely diabetic, and a hundred pounds overweight. She could be pleasant enough when she wanted to be. I still think of her when I hesitate to go out on a rainy day. "We're neither sugar nor salt," she would say, lifting her huge body from the front seat of my car. But she leached attention.

Evelyn had a way of calling up on the busiest days and saying, "What you doing?" I learned to brace myself for the next question. Was she out of catfood? Or dangerously ill and in need of a ride to the emergency room? She had a way of making the most ridiculous requests sound earnest and the most serious needs seem self-indulgent. I knew that if I said "No," she would call Alice, and that whatever either of us did, we would spend an hour on the phone later trying to decide if it had been right. I will never forget the night she called to ask if my husband Gael would come and give her a blessing because she had just eaten a dozen Dunkin' Donuts she had paid a Dover taxi driver to deliver. Looking back, I am amazed at the total ineffectiveness of our efforts either to help her or to keep her demands within bounds.

When Evelyn died, visiting teaching became less strenuous, but it was no more satisfying. Much of the time I was without a partner. There were few active families in our end of the ward, and the women teamed with me had a way of disappearing. With five children and a seminary class to teach, I had plenty to keep me busy, even without seminar papers to write. Besides, I now knew there were some problems that no loaf of bread could solve. The names on my visiting teaching list grew increasingly gray.

About that time, a high councilor spoke in our ward on the subject of motivation. He said that sometimes we fail to achieve our goals because we expect too much of ourselves. His solution was to replace grandiose plans with small, easily attainable objectives. He had acquired the habit of daily scripture reading, for example, by ignoring the admonition to read at least a chapter a day. He vowed to read one verse. "Now anybody can do that," he said. Because his goal was so ridiculously easy, he almost always achieved it, and most of the time he did more. For some reason, sitting there in the back of the chapel, I started thinking about visiting teaching. One person on my list really needed a visit. If I reached her every month, maybe I should consider that I had done my job. Because the Relief Society secretary was already convinced that I never went, the report wouldn't matter much anyway. I felt a wonderful sense of relief.

Myrtle Johnson lived in a trailer park eight miles west of Durham with two enormous gray cats named Sinbad and Sir Francis. Though past seventy, she still did housework for several well-to-do families in the area. Myrtle was a native of Maine and had lived much of her life in New Hampshire, though she had spent six or seven years in Colorado, where she joined the Church. While still in the West, she had received her endowment in the Salt Lake Temple. To my knowledge, she had never attended our ward. Probably she had been too busy just trying to stay alive. Not long after returning to New Hampshire from Colorado, she had suffered a stroke. Though she was now back at work cleaning houses, I doubt if she had enough energy left over, or enough gas for her old car, to drive the twenty miles to Portsmouth on Sunday.

Myrtle had been married and widowed three times, though she had been separated from her first husband, the father of her children, at the time he was killed by a hit-and-run driver. She always spoke of her second husband with a special softness. He had been diagnosed as terminally ill not long after their marriage. I think he was the one she hoped to claim for eternity, though the third husband, Mr. Johnson, had joined the Church when she did.

Myrtle was a small, brown-eyed woman, enormously spunky and full of fun. She loved nice clothes, and though most of hers were hand-me-downs from various employers, she took good care of them and wore them with pride. Her eyeglasses, with their filigreed metallic frames that turned up at the temples, were years out of date, but on Myrtle they looked stylish. Her tiny trailer was a riotous tangle of house plants, crocheted poodles, and ceramic knickknacks, so many knickknacks and so much trailing ivy that the unlit Christmas lights hanging around the window all year were scarcely visible. On the sofa, which was covered with bath towels to protect it from the cats, was a faded satin pillow stamped "Mother."

This clutter of a lifetime came alive in Myrtle's talk. Within a few months I felt that I knew the "Bair boys" who had introduced her to the Church, and I could picture Myrtle in her "temple class" somewhere in Colorado, determined to outdo the couples who had been members all their lives. "I made it!" she would say. As she told me the story of her stroke, I could see her lying on a newly scrubbed floor, just out of reach of the telephone, praying that her employer would come home in time to save her life, and I could imagine the fire in her eyes as she hoisted weights in the therapy room at the Wentworth-Douglas hospital, determined to regain the use of her arm. Myrtle was proud of her recovery, but most nights she was too exhausted to do anything but feed her cats and go to bed. I don't think she ever neglected her tiny yard, however. There wasn't much sun in the Pine Knoll Trailer Park, but from May to October, her faded red trailer was bordered with flowers.

A year or so after I started visiting Myrtle, she decided to give up work. She hoped that by getting rid of her car, she would be able to make do on Social Security. It was soon obvious that she needed to get out of her trailer far more than she needed my visit. I asked the Relief Society president to make her my companion. Once a month we spent a morning together, visiting the two or three Mormon sisters in Durham, then stopping at the grocery store so Myrtle could pick up anything she had forgotten on her weekly trip to Exeter with the senior citizens van. She always rushed through her shopping, respectful of my need to get my daughter Amy home for her nap.

Before long I was picking her up for Sunday School and then after a while for sacrament meeting as well. Sometimes she stayed at our house between meetings, always bringing something for our meal—scalloped oysters, a "surprise meat loaf," or an apple crisp. Because Myrtle lived in the opposite direction from our house to the church, picking her up for meetings added a full hour to our Sunday driving. For some reason it didn't feel like a chore. Even our children, always restless in the car, enjoyed the ride. The stories she told along the highway made me feel at home in northern New England in a way I never had before. She put names to the flowers growing in the waste places along the road, and as we crossed the many bridges between Durham and Portsmouth, she almost made me, a landlubber, want to climb into a boat and go flounder fishing or oystering. On cold Sunday mornings, she would talk about ice fishing. She worried that her son-in-law Emery had decided she was too old to sit with him all night in a fish shack in the middle of the pond. She was sure she could do it.

Sometimes she talked about her childhood in Maine. We could see her father coming into the house with a gunnysack full of lobsters while her mother got the big kettle boiling. I was never sure whether it was her real father who brought the lobsters or "Father Pike," the foster father she lived with for a time. Our children loved to hear Myrtle tell about the morning she caught Father Pike, who was a devout Quaker, swearing at the cow. When Myrtle tried the same language the next morning, Mother Pike washed her mouth out with soap.

Even the deprivation of Myrtle's childhood took on richness as she talked. We heard about her years in the Augusta Home for Girls. "My sister and I weren't in the part where the bad girls went," she said. "We hadn't done anything wrong. We were just—well, you know—underprivileged." When Myrtle and her sister outgrew the Home, they found their way to Newburyport, Massachusetts, where Myrtle got a job in a factory assembling electric fuses. She quit work when she married, but by the time World War II began, her husband had been killed, and she was supporting her four living children, working as a waitress most of the time until the Portsmouth Naval shipyard opened its gates to women.

Her job at the shipyard was the apex of Myrtle's working life. She loved to tell how she worked her way up from the hydraulic press to the ten-ton crane, losing the ends of two fingers in the process. She would have stayed at the shipyard if she could have. The pay was the best she had ever had, and there was an exhilaration in being able to do a job no woman had done before. As she told about her work, Myrtle would lean forward in her seat, her hands poised above imaginary levers, demonstrating how, sitting in a cab high above the unfinished ships, she had guided huge sheets of steel toward the workers below. An inch or two in the wrong direction, and the men could have been crushed.

Myrtle showed no bitterness, however, about losing her job after the war. "We were just glad to see the men come home," she said. I understood her feelings, yet I couldn't help wondering what her retirement would have been like if she had spent thirty years working in the shipyard rather than piecing together a living doing housework and practical nursing. Although Myrtle worked hard all her life, she had no pension of any kind, and her Social Security was minimal. I am sure that her children would have contributed more than they did to her support, but she was fiercely independent, and there was real tension with at least one daughter. Finding it hard to pay her utilities, Myrtle tried babysitting a few days a week, but her trailer was small and her patience with young mothers limited.

One day she told me she had found the perfect solution to her financial problems. She had heard somewhere that the State Welfare Department was looking for families willing to share their homes with the elderly. By sleeping on the sofa, she could provide the private bedroom the regulations demanded. I looked at her with amazement, but she was so determined that I eventually wrote the character reference she needed. I happened to be at her house when the social worker came to "inspect" the premises. It was obvious that the paper regulations meant nothing; the few welfare spaces in New

Hampshire nursing homes were so limited that the state was willing to accept any private home they could get.

Myrtle's first patient, who was only supposed to be there a few days because she was somewhat more disabled than the guidelines required, had lost a leg to diabetes. Myrtle managed the special diet well enough, and I think felt satisfaction in again performing what was clearly practical nursing, but she worried about the lifting. She also missed coming to meetings. Because the woman was depressed, Myrtle was afraid to leave her alone. We were all relieved when this woman left and a "permanent" boarder arrived.

I think the new woman's name was Sarah, although Myrtle always called her The Old Lady. She was over ninety, incredibly wizened, and senile. She had lived alone off in the woods somewhere without plumbing or electricity until a few months before when the neighbors, fearing she would freeze to death, had called an ambulance and sent her to the Rochester Hospital, where she stayed until her Medicare ran out. Now she was Myrtle's problem.

The Old Lady was a tough bird, as Myrtle would have said, but she was obviously confused and frightened by her recent moves. One day she threatened to take out her six-shooter and blow Myrtle's brains out. "I know your kind," she said. "I see a string of men coming into this trailer every day for their pleasure and not yours."

Myrtle was angry at the State of New Hampshire but genuinely concerned about her new charge and reluctant to abandon her. The welfare office kept telling her that they hoped to find a place in a nursing home if Myrtle could just hold on for a few more days. One night my husband responded to an emergency call from Myrtle who couldn't get The Old Lady off the commode. As I remember it, she had locked her hands on the arms of her portable commode and refused to move. When Gael arrived, she became perfectly docile. "I'm all yours," she said. "You can do anything you want with me."

Finally Myrtle did the only thing she could do—call the ambulance and send The Old Lady back to the Rochester Hospital. The State found her a place in a Hampton nursing home the next day; three days later, she died. For Myrtle that was the end of the Share-a-Home program. I think she had learned her lesson, yet in one respect it was a bitter one. If she no longer had the ability to care for old ladies, she might become one.

One spring morning, Myrtle phoned to tell me how upset she was that the senior citizens van was not going to come that day. The weather was warm, and she had been counting on a trip to the nursery in Exeter to get some things she needed for her garden. I listened to her complaint and, for a second, thought I was hearing Evelyn Johnson. Myrtle didn't actually ask me to drive her to Exeter, but I knew she was hoping I would. As I searched for the words to tell her I was busy, a quiet voice came into my head. "Myrtle has never taken advantage of you. She wouldn't have called if she hadn't been desperately low."

Half an hour later, Amy and I picked her up. As we drove toward the nursery, I began to think of the empty planter box on the deck outside my bedroom window. When her own shopping was done, Myrtle helped me choose annuals and hanging ivy, then came home and helped me plant them. We laughed together as we fixed lunch. The ivy lasted through two seasons, wintering in my loft. When Myrtle was gone, her green thumb sustained me.

Not everybody saw Myrtle as I did. Certainly she made friends in the ward, but I think some people, at least until they got to know her, were a bit afraid of her. She said what she thought. Maybe that's what I liked about her. My mother was a spunky soul like Myrtle, but we were too bound up with one another emotionally to develop an easygoing relationship. I feared my mother's disapproval in much the same way Myrtle's daughter seems to have feared hers. Myrtle had no doubt been a superb cleaning lady—all her coiled energy would go into whatever she did—but I'm not sure I would have wanted to expose my domestic behavior to her discerning eye. It amused and shocked me to hear her tell about the time she informed a family counselor in Durham that she would no longer clean his house if he didn't stop swearing at his children. Because Myrtle and I had no obligations to each other that were not freely chosen, I could love her unconditionally and she me.

One Sunday morning I called to tell her that we would be a few minutes late picking her up for stake conference. I knew that she wanted to go because I had talked with her on Friday. She had been busy planning a dinner she was having for one of the couples in the ward. When she didn't answer, I felt a sense of foreboding, though I dismissed it, thinking she was probably in the shower. She wasn't at the window when we arrived at her house, nor did she respond to my knock on her door. Instinctively, I went to her bedroom window at the end of the trailer. I could see her lying on the bed in a folded position, perfectly still.

When Jean Harford and I went to the funeral home on Monday morning to dress Myrtle in her temple clothes, the mortician told us he thought she had died Saturday afternoon about two. He apologized for the condition of the body. There were deep seams across her shoulders where he had pulled in her arms to get her into a restful position for burial. He was a friendly man, like most in his profession, and he chatted with us in a matter-of-fact way, attempting, I'm sure, to ease our difficult task. Yet he hadn't even bothered to drape Myrtle's body with a sheet.

She lay, pink and bloated on the white enamel table, her face made up, her hair perfectly curled, and all the imperfections of her useless body exposed. I had not known Myrtle's fingers were so arthritic or her toes so gnarled. Imbedded in her flesh just above the right breast was a curious little white thing, like an old underwear button, or the valve on an inflatable toy.

As Jean and I eased the garments onto her stiffened limbs, I felt a sweet feeling of love and deep sorrow for the indignities and the injustices of this world. Many years later the diary of the Maine midwife, Martha Ballard, gave me a name for that experience. She called it "the last office of friendship."

WHAT TIME IS IT?

DURING TWENTY-ONE DAYS in Russia, we never knew what time it was. Our inner timepieces were confounded by crisscrossing nine of the eleven time zones in the Union of Soviet Socialist Republics. Too, it was June, when nights were one-third as long as we were used to in Utah. Most of all, centuries were confused—1984 (the year of our visit) could have been 1734 with abacus adding in uzbekistan or 1894 in a subway of mahogany and chandeliers in Moscow.

Time was of the essence. A different kind of essence.

My time with Russia had begun in the summer of 1983 when David Freed, recently retired first cellist with the Utah symphony, called me about joining him for a traveling performance of his Bach and my poems to celebrate "kinship among nations," sponsored by the Utah Arts Council. I liked the idea.

My generation four decades before had responded very differently to the dropping of the bomb than I respond now. In 1945 we wanted the war ended, with the loss, of course, of as few of our own as possible. Now, forty years later, I wanted nothing to do with that bomb or the proliferation of its progeny. But why? When the change in me? I needed to write the poems "to explain me to myself." I wrote six "Considerations" about my learning what war and peace mean.

Written to be read aloud, the next year *How Much for the Earth?* was published by Utahns United in a limited edition chapbook. It was being translated at Dartmouth by Walter Arndt into German and Russian as our program took the poems and Bach across the state.

After a reading in 1984 as part of BYU's Peace among Nations Week, Russian professor Gary Browning commented to me, "You should take your poems to the Soviet Union, Emma Lou. Poetry is a second language there. Poets are heroes. And peace is on their minds in a different way than it's on ours."

Two months later, by every kind of serendipity and good fortune, I left for the USSR with thirty-six others on an education exchange tour under the guidance of Drs. Kent Robson and Lynn Eliason, professors of philosophy and languages at Utah State University. They were six-time visitors to the Soviet Union and fluent in its language and history.

My poems went with me in both English and Russian. The book in translation was like having a second visa, one that people read aloud from, nodded and smiled at. In Russia, the poems eased me through customs in Moscow, were handled and read by scarf-clad women in a packed church, were part of a reading in a dining car as we spent four and a half days and nights on the Trans-Siberian Railway zooming through the surprising beauties of Siberia and its collectives tucked among the Ural Mountains, the Taiga Forest, the lush fields and meadows along the Volga. They were yet to introduce me to people of various ages and occupations in modern Tashkent near Mongolia, in ancient Samarkand on the border of Afghanistan, and to others who would alter my conception of war and allegiance to peace.

I had not known what to expect. My knowledge of contemporary Russia was *Peter and the Wolf* and *Dr. Zhivago*, the names and fates of emigrés and dissidents gleaned from newspapers, and hearsay. Everything had been as surprising as the beauty of Siberia, or seeing only one gas station in Moscow, a city of seven million, a line-up for it like the queuing in the butcher shop for narrow veins of lean in great slabs of fat. We had brushed our teeth in mineral water and Pepsi. We had heard Verdi in the Kremlin. We had breakfasted on reindeer, cucumbers, and caviar. Nothing about the trip had been ordinary. Especially those people I had gone there to meet, did meet, without limit or surveillance, with the group and on my own.

But my most surprising adventure with a Soviet, the poems, and the idea of peace came in Irkutsk, Siberia, a college town of six hundred thousand. Not quite two weeks gone of our three, we sat in a vast mahogany room draped with flags in the city's House of Friendship. We were going to learn about education. The Soviets had been obviously proud of their accomplishments. Moscow University, with thirty thousand students, was typical of huge complexes of institutes, universities, and schools in every city and republic. The 3 percent literacy before the 1917 revolution was now less than 3 percent illiteracy. Our instructor was to be a member of the Communist party, one of a 5 percent ruling minority, and we were prepared for the party line, something we'd not been given anywhere along the way.

Then Valentina—Valya to her friends—appeared. Stylish in a summer print, poised on slim high heels, she had the bearing of a model. Blonde-coiffed and vibrant, she spoke with a clipped British accent and an ingenuous warmth that disarmed and surprised us.

She introduced herself as a teacher in the Academy of Sciences. She taught English to scientists, businessmen, artists, government leaders.

She told of growing up in a home where her mother was Christian, her father Communist.

"Who won out?" we asked.

"You see here the mixture," she said, pointing to herself. She told of carrying in her head Bible stories and Russian fairy tales to schools where the state was the only religion, of being the only one in her family of five living children to join the Communist party, of celebrating religious holidays with her mother, until recently, in secret. She told how her mother at eighty-three, the biggest influence in her life, was still unable to sign her name. But she had helped her children with algebra, mysteriously coming up with the answers, and she saw to it that they all had advanced educations.

She told how hard it was to get into the Communist party, how much work it took to stay there, that religion was never taught in school, only in homes where an older generation might still have a Bible.

"What about peace? Do you have any ways of working for peace?"

She told of committees who met in that very House of Friendship, of children's peace groups started by hearing of similar children's groups in San Francisco who were influencing thinking between generations. Suddenly she said, "If I had three wishes, you know what the first would be?" She held up one finger, her voice softening. "For peace."

"And the other two wishes?"

She put her other two fingers up one at a time. "For peace. For peace." No one spoke for a moment.

Many other questions were asked, answered.

With the bus waiting to take us to our hotel and lunch and then to our plane for Tashkent, I talked to Valentina, told of peace groups I was part of as a nonpolitical person: Utahns United against the Nuclear Arms Race, Women Concerned about Nuclear War, of people at home who felt exactly as she did about wishes one, two, and three.

By now everyone was in the bus waiting, as usual, for me. Was there a way she could come to our hotel for lunch, to talk further? No, but why didn't I ride with her in her car? Minutes later, I was in the passenger's seat. The bus left and Valentina slid in, took hold of the top of the steering wheel with both hands, flung her head down on it and said, "I was *so* nervous!"

We laughed. "I have done this only twice," she confided, "answered these questions by non-Soviets. I am a teacher of English."

We laughed again. An hour and a half later, now in the hotel lobby, we were still talking. About the party, yes, and about our governments, nuclear arming, the Olympics. But more about our daughters, my five, her two.

"What does your husband do?" she asked.

"He's a real estate broker," I tried, then laughed again trying to explain the exchange of land and property for a fee—as impossible for her to imagine as a credit card or a grocery store aisle full of frozen TV dinners.

She invited me to dinner across the river in her apartment. Was her apartment better than it might have been because she was a Communist party official? No, she smiled.

Out of my journal fell a picture of my whole family—all seventeen of us—at our last daughter's wedding. "All yours?" she asked, astonished. I nodded, pointed out daughters and husbands, grandchildren. "Do they all dress alike?" she asked.

"Only for that night—the wedding party, you know," I explained, then, embarrassed at the apparent extravagance, "These two daughters—they sewed the dresses. They will wear them again."

She looked long at the picture, then asked, "Could I keep it?"

"Of course," I said. "The family will be yours in America."

We exchanged addresses, hers in my journal in her exotic hand with a dozen others, mine in the book I inscribed to her, along with a tape of my poems in English and the Russian version, and an article on Russia by Gary Browning from *BYU Today* that I had stashed in my suitcase and circulated among our group.

By now others had come into the lobby from lunch. Could she come to Utah under the sponsorship of a university? She might but would need a formal invitation. We promised to write.

The group trickled toward the bus. Valentina pulled my little, stuffed red roller bag through the lobby, across the asphalt parking, seeming as reluctant as I was to let go. At the door of the bus we hugged, familial as old friends longing for time, kissed cheeks like sisters.

In my seat I thought, "This has to be what I came for. This hope."

A retired chemical engineer leaned toward where I sat. All along he had been a man on whom nothing was lost, a man going home to report to his high priests' quorum what he had seen. He said, "Isn't she amazing? But so much like us in the Church—unique and genuine until we start spouting the party line."

I knew he was right. She had changed dramatically when we had asked questions she had only secondhand answers for. I knew too that we Americans had the right to be different, could use our God-given agency, protected by a constitution and tradition that said so. But I thought too how we limit ourselves, victimized by the same stereotyping, acquiescence to conformity, suspicious of differences.

That encounter with Valentina and her country convinced me that the possibility for peace among any of us—within our cozy Utah boundaries or across the skitterish globe—is in ourselves. Since coming home after my time with the Valentinas and three cordial Sergeis of the Soviet Union, I have heard over and over, "But you can't trust your experience. The people are not the government."

I know. But they are. Just as we are. And every exchange, even the small ones, can make a difference. However, we can find to exercise our agency and free ourselves of cliché either in speech or expectation through personal enlightenment, the closer we can come to freeing the world from suspicion and ultimate destruction.

Back home more than four months, by Halloween I had wondered why I had not heard from Valentina. Three of us had written to her (two were deans from the University of Utah who had also been on the trip) and asked if she could come, had even set dates as the USIA had suggested we do. Had there been reprisals for her being so friendly with us?

I decided to call her in her Irkutsk, Siberia.

Three times the operator called me back, trying, each time at a different number. By then we were friends, him determined. "Siberia! We'll get her." Then, "Hey, we've got Valentina on the line!"

She sounded no farther away than Provo. "Are you really calling from Utah? What a treat! What a surprise!" she exclaimed.

I had an echo, could ask questions only slowly without overlapping what she was saying. Between every remark, "Such a treat! Such a surprise—from Utah!"

"I start a new class November 15," she said. And you must know—every student reads your poems aloud in English. Then I tell them to listen to the tape to see how they should sound."

My poems? Read by those businessmen, government officials, artists, scientists—people who just might have a say about something?

"And your family," she said, "tell them I love them. That they are seen everywhere."

Of course I loved her, loved what she was telling me, felt my conceptions totally validated. "Has it changed what you say about America and Americans, as you travel around speaking and teaching, having met all of us?" I asked. "You can't imagine how meeting you has changed everything for *me*—for all of us on our tour."

"Oh, yes," she said. "In fact, I'm so glad you called today. Did you have Halloween yesterday?"

"No," I said. "It's today."

"What time is it there?" She was smiling across the thousands of miles.

"Nearly one in the afternoon."

She laughed. "It's nearly four in the morning here."

"I will tell all my students, my family of your call," she said. "You would be happy to know that on your Halloween I took a program about America to my fifteen-year-old daughter's class. I carved a jack-o-lantern from a pumpkin and told them about all of you. Could you come again?"

We talked for eighteen minutes—thirty-seven dollars on my AT&T bill a month later. What value in Russian-United States currency that connection? I hung up aglow.

Yes, I'll continue to write my congresspeople, talk to my family and friends, join where I can to hold hands with others of hope and more than intention. I will encourage exchange, formal and otherwise, root for the re-instigation of programs canceled by unwitting political punishment of the wrong people.

I will declare my certainty that human beings deserve more credit than we give ourselves. That only through hope and willingness to find out about each other can the earth and all it is worth be saved.

I will love my country as I never could have, its buoyancy, brashness, entrepreneuring. I will get teary at the "Star Spangled Banner" and do what I can to let my grandchildren know why. Better because I have been to the Soviet Union, seen its repression, its lines, its burial places, its adoration of Mother Russia.

Beyond any of what I will *do*, I will cherish in a grateful heart having been forever altered, enriched, blessed by those twenty-one days of wondering "What time is it?"

ABOUT CONSIDERING

Consider is the word
the bishops used last fall
as counsel to their people concerning buildup
for a war by holocaust. Consider.

A not-bad word, considering.
It makes you grateful you exist and can—
consider, that is.
You pay attention, you notice.
You want to be worthy of considering, consideration.

That's after all how you decide what hurts or makes you happy.
In this of all matters, it matters.

Given the idea, it is not a question of either words
or numbers, but something that will keep us humans
in business, the considering to which God bows,
to which theories of matter and mattering
come second if at all.

Relativity. I understand that's where it started.
Einstein and his "energy equals mass times the speed of light
squared."

To consider must be relative as well.
Relative to all I ever learned
in coming to this moment when speed of light
squares off against the speed of time.

And what I would consider
in this late season is: to calculate whether we peacemakers
shall inherit or destroy
this blessed earth.

(First of eight poems from *How Much for the Earth?*)

Emma Lou Thayne • 1983

CONSIDERING THE END

So finally I consider only life: The holocaust ahead
would leave no one behind
to question how we happened not to happen
in any moment but our tragic own.

I have only one voice, one language,
one set of memories to look back on,
a thousand impulses to look ahead
if I will
if there is time
to consider:
How much for the earth?
what would I keep?

Blue mountains against a black sky,
Smiles exchanged so well we do not know our ages or conditions.

Snow melted, leaves moving again,
In a voice, rain finding its way to the stream.

Heat rising like wands from the desert,
A cold drink, the touch of hair enough all by itself.

First apricot pickle sharp, a phone ringing on time,
Lights going on, wanting them off for the dark.

A song flooded with memory, smell of pinon in fire, onion in stew,
A dancer watched like a child, a child in flight like a dancer.

Hot soup, hot bath, hot air to take to the canyon,
Aging slowly from the bones outward, time to pick and choose.

A wooden spoon, the white whisper of a needle in cloth,
Laughing like tossed water, like skis on snow.

Smell of soap, hot animal. An apple, crisp. A ball hit,
Tongue of a lover, dream of a dead mother stroking our cheek.

An idea, the Pieta, the Hand of God, a word, a prayer,
The word, the earth far from without form and void.

The earth created and not destroyed. If altered,
not back to darkness upon the face of the deep.

You, me, combinations of color and sound,
The spirit of God moving upon the waters.

A child born, an aunt with reason to blow draw blow,
A celebration for the end of war. A new generation inevitable.

The coming of sun because it is good.
A world alive for a blue door to open onto.

A candle, a kiss, eyes meeting. Holding.
Life—to consider.

Then no more considering, hypothesizing, tolerating.

No litmus-paper ending in a cosmic Petri dish.

No more silence.

For the earth?

For the life in me, in you,
I say Yes. Yes thank you. Yes.

In your breath fused with mine
Even ashes stir and glow.

It's time. It's time we said together
Yes to life. To ashes, simply No.

GOING WITH GOD:
VALENTINA'S STORY

In December 1945, Russia and the United States were still allies. Valentina Alexandra was 8 years old and living with her family off the leavings of potatoes in frozen fields around her village near Lake Baikal in Siberia. Her most vivid memory—being hungry. And cold. This is my telling of her story.

"GO WITH GOD," HER mother said as she always did.

Valentina Alexandra, eight, and her brother Vladimir, six, pulled on the mittens and hats their mother had knitted and headed their boots to the potato field. This one was beyond the city with its wooden houses, over a mile away. They were silent. Any talk would turn white like the sky. They slapped their hands and would rather have run to get there quicker, but they knew to breathe slowly so their nostrils would not stick together and their eyes water onto their cheeks.

It was November, 1946, in Irkutsk, Siberia. The River Angara had started to freeze a week ago. The rutted road to the fields was ice-hard as well.

"We must be fast today," Valentina said.

Vladimir only nodded, knowing like her that almost before they arrived at the field, darkness would fall and stay for more than twice as long as the day, forever its own creature. At home, the chimney of the lamp would be white over the black of the burning wick. His brother, Kesha, and his three sisters would bed down in the loft above the brick stove. There it was warm for the early part of the night, and Valentina would be first to be in bed to hear the fairy tales their mother would tell from the kitchen, always about tables heaped with food. It was not fair that today he had to be the one to come with Valentina for potatoes.

The children moved together by habit, up and down the rows. Here, there, a frozen potato, half a one, missed in last year's harvest on the collective farm. From the whole field only eleven in the knit bag. Only enough for two days with seven at the table. Perhaps—and Valentina's stomach tightened in anticipation—perhaps the Lubamodrovs across the road in their blue wooden house with carved wooden lace around the windows would give their potato peels—sometimes thick on purpose—and her mother would fry them right on the iron top of the stove. Lately her mother never mentioned the butter or fish oil she used to fry in before the war.

Coming home, Valentina could not remember not being hungry. Vladimir, as always, was first to the door. But Valentina knew before he opened it that nothing was as it had been. Her nostrils opened even in the cold to something, something pungent and tingly. It made her mouth water and her stomach contract. What?

At the stove in her red-flowered babushka, her mother smiled a broad smile. In the black frying pan, what she stirred sputtered and sizzled. Steam rose and took over the room in a fragrance definitely not potatoes. Into Valentina's wide eyes came the blur of tears. Like those in her mother's, even as she smiled. She could not have said why. Then there was her father, usually so serious, also smiling. His job in the mine was exhausting. He was a communist who must be an atheist. What if anyone saw the icons, Jesus Christ and his mother Mary painted on wood, kept hidden from him by her mother in the drawer where flour used to be? What if anyone saw the family when he was at the mine, saying prayers on Christmas as if Grandfather Frost were not enough to celebrate the New Year. What if her mother said it too loud when any of them started out from home—"Go with God"?

Now here he was, her wiry father, smiling and opening his arms to the stove and her mother, then turning to open his arms to them.

"Sausage," he said. "Sausage. Today delivered to the mine and distributed. For all of us some."

"From where?" Valentina wondered, must have said aloud.

"Do you remember the film *Meeting at the Elbe* that we have seen many times?"

Of course, she remembered—in the half-roofed mining club, the film. Russian soldiers and American soldiers, allies, embracing, laughing, some crying. The end of the Germans. The war soon over.

"You remember the brothering?" His eyes were shining. She liked that word he always used about the meeting at the Elbe River flowing to the North Sea. "Well, today—the brothering. This sausage. And on the train soon more, other items. From America."

Two days later he took them all to see the green train in the station, hissing, men pounding with huge hammers at the iron of the wheels and the great rods that moved them. From a stack of goods her father was handed the folds of an enormous piece of heavy fabric. "American gifts," he said.

Her mother instructed Valentina and her two sisters to hold its other three corners, to spread it out. Puzzled at the broad rose-colored square, big as their kitchen, bumpy with knots, they touched its fringes and looked to each other. What could it be? No matter, her mother said.

Out of it she made dresses for Valentina Alexandra and her two sisters, Luda, ten, and Masha, thirteen. The last dress was passed down to Valentina nearly ten years after the meeting at the Elbe. She still called it her dress from America.

Or, as her mother insisted, from God.

That was 1945. In June 1984, Valentina, then forty-six though looking thirty-five, had talked to us as head of the department of foreign languages at the Academy of Sciences in Irkutsk, Siberia, to answer questions about Soviet education for our group of thirty-eight Americans on our U.S. education exchange tour.

In the fall of 1987, Valentina came for eighty-four days to Utah. Miracle enough her being here, let alone, as she said, "by a stroke of luck," during the weeks prior to the Reagan-Gorbachev summit, the historic once-upon-a-time when *perestroika, glasnost, arms reduction,* and even *peace* were words enjoyed like hugs at a family reunion.

It had taken three years of what even she called red tape on her side, two of the same over here arranging for her visit.

But here she was, an amazing emissary, living in Salt Lake City, in our corner bedroom. In her black shawl with its bright borders, her embroidered red felt skirt, and white puff-sleeved blouse, she was a Russian fairy tale herself, a nest doll, a *Matreshka*. "You never told us she was so beautiful," came from both men and women.

Still loyal to her communist homeland, infused with its "from all according to ability; to all according to need," she took in America as she took her notes—with sparkling attention and ingenuous curiosity. Valentina sitting ecstatic behind the wheel in one of acres of shiny cars at a mega-dealership, then telling later about "garage clubs" in Irkutsk where owners of the few cars park and lounge with their TV and vodka. She is not only a nondrinker but the only woman member in her garage club. The Soviet wives ask her, "Just what do they do in there all that time?"

In an OB/GYN exam and diagnosis at the University of Utah Health Sciences Center: "Your medicine is so advanced, so comfortable. But how much does it cost? Ours is free to all." But "No mammogram there—except perhaps in Moscow. And mostly no birth control, only abortion, an average of nine per woman in a lifetime."

At Clayton Jr. High a line-up—to her a "queue"—to vote in a local primary in a striped booth where a woman and her husband might vote for different candidates. Valentina: "We elect our officials at a local level, and Gorbachev is initiating a multiple candidate ballot." The persistent hope for the perestroika she had seen taking root but being resisted "by conservatives" at home.

In a newspaper newsroom where anyone could walk in anytime, without invitation, she observed, "Glasnost is making news available to us that we never had—and sooner." Irkutsk had not heard about Chernobyl until days after the nuclear disaster.

In our papers while she was here, a stock market crash, the denial of a seat to a Supreme Court nominee, an eventually aborted attempt by Aryan Nations to take their hatred to the radio. This along with earth-shaking details on Raisa's wardrobe and Nancy's one-upmanship.

She pored over everything my history-major husband, Mel (her happy clipping service), daily provided, rationalized to us about Refuseniks and, even as she talked total equality at home, complained about no positions of major authority for women in the USSR.

At the congeniality of service and salespeople, of even a friendly dentist: "In my country, a customer is an annoyance." On leaving Dan's newest supermarket: "Tell me, how do millionaires live?"

She went to a football game, saw Gershwin, heard the Utah Symphony and the Tabernacle Choir. She sat up late to watch Robert Redford or Judy Garland on video. She beat the best in our family at Ping-Pong, saw Martina and Chrissy play tennis at the Special Events Center at the University of Utah, fell in love with my word processor.

Because she loved handiwork, she spoke at a Relief Society quilting day, was given a quilt, and arranged flowers at a wedding, working with the expert. She climbed up a ladder and repaired our ancient Jerusalem lamp with black tape. In jeans and a T-shirt, looking like a teenager with a long blonde ponytail, she ironed even her socks and underwear—ours, too! More than informative, like someone from another planet herself, she was never not a treat.

But what stayed with us and will go home with her has much more to do with another connection beyond any ability, congeniality, or introduction to abundance. She talked about her mother "with her Russian soul. She believed in soul and believed in people, and I think it actually helped us a lot to understand how the world goes around and how people live."

Virginia Woolf knew about it: "Without soul, we are inclined to satire rather than to compassion, to scrutiny of society rather than understanding of individuals themselves."

Compassion and understanding were Valentina's luggage and ID, satire and scrutiny what she was used to dealing with. Groups could arrive suspicious, find themselves listening, asking questions, fascinated. Every preconception of a Soviet woman, a communist, seeping away, people begged for more, kept her talking for hours.

"What if she is KGB?" some skeptics still wondered.

Valentina with language and soul her secrets? But suppose by some wild chance she were? What would we have chosen not to send home with her—or have her leave here?

No. Contradictory as she was beguiling, she was actual, would last. With rapt university students, she reviewed Pushkin's poetry, Siberian Rasputin's controversial environmental stories, Vampilov's plays of apathy and corruption, even Pasternak's Christian philosophies, compared translations with out-of-school members of the literature class that overflowed into Grethe Peterson's living room.

She talked to a class in journalism, became defensive when asked about card-carrying privileges. To insistence of KGB presence in her homeland, snapped, "Rubbish!"

She visited the Missionary Training Center at BYU, wanted to see it be "lighter—language is learned best when it's fun." She brought tapes from the Archbishop of Northern Siberia, slides of Siberian artists, songs from children in elementary grades to teach her classes with. She wrote the words to "Home on the Range" in her journal and fell in love with "America" as sung by Barbra Streisand, sang it with tears about "the charmed silence" at the cabin or, dismayed, about the waste of throwing out whole trays of plastic tableware at the University's Union cafeteria.

She was dedicated to taking back that crash course in American English for her scientists: "They don't want to learn British English like mine, from tapes. American English is the language of science, and they need to understand and speak it." She savored the sound of phrases, her favorite new words: *frolic, serendipity, felicity, entrepreneur, crepuscular, antelope, "Jacuzzying," plethora.* "I'm being spoiled and corrupted, you know," as she drove my car or put on makeup.

She taught us a Russian children's song—"Let there always be sunshine, let there always be blue skies, let there always be Mama, let there always be me." That and "America" she liked to have audiences join her in singing. And often when she and

I finished a talk together, we took turns, I in English, she translating in Russian, reading lines from a poem I'd written that September for women peace delegates come to Salt Lake from Botswana, Thailand, New Zealand, and the Netherlands.

Woman of Another World

You, woman of a different tongue,
awaken me.
Speak in the language of light that flutters between us.
Open my heart to your dailiness;
give voice to your fears and celebrations
as you wonder at mine.

Your family becomes me,
the substance of what you believe
colors my view.
You take me on.
Here, here is my hand.

Filled with yours
it pulses with new hope
and a fierce longing
to let the light that guides us both
tell me where to be.

At the end of nearly three months, she was exhausted—and overwhelmed. She had talked to maybe more than 1,500 people here, would in the first week home talk to 20,000 there. Packing her way-past-stuffed bags to leave, she said, "All this everyone has given me. But more, the outpouring of spirit. Like your prayers, personal and sacred. And like the quilt, so many stitches, and each a piece of a person to take home."

She left herself and treasures as well, Lithuanian amber rings and bracelets, badges and "sweets" for the children she entranced, Moskovskaya vodka "not for you Mormons!" laughing, "I never knew when to offer it." Even her black shawl and her red skirt she gave away. People asked how she could bear going back to the "hardships, the repression." I had longed at the end of only three weeks of fascination in her country to come home to my mountains, my people; after nearly three months, she needed "to get back to her lovely Siberia." We both decided, "It will take silence to subdue the rush, Siberia to grant the holy hush."

That last day, checking our throw-away mail—the many ads that she loved to pore over—"Emma Lou, come and see! The gift from America! This is it!"

In her hand was a brochure from ZCMI about a white sale, on the back of it, fringed, nubbed, rose-colored, the mystery from her childhood solved. "See—this is what my mother made our dresses of—a bedspread! It must have been the size for a king."

There it was, the Bates spread like I'd slept under in 1945 in my room on Crystal Avenue waiting for my brother to come home from war. The connections—over oceans and borders, ideologies and backgrounds. I would miss Valentina as I missed my girlhood, the zest, the naivete, the openheartedness. But the fairy tale had come true. And her translation of America I would treasure as she must mine of her Siberia. In a new language of light.

The light that is with Valentina exists wherever the opportunity arises to find it in others. It is what any traveling—by conventional means or by soul—is all about.

ABIGAIL

THIS ESSAY IS FOR Abigail Carr, age three. She is a sturdy little girl with serious eyes under brows as dark and definite as a grownup's. Her wayward pigtails require six barrettes, in various colors. Abigail's older brothers—Benjamin, Abraham, and Isaac—have similar cowlicks, though theirs have been tamed with crew cuts. Their dad, who is a university professor, says his colleagues think he named his sons for Benjamin Franklin, Abraham Lincoln, and Isaac Newton. The boys know better.

Abigail, too, will soon know her Biblical heritage if she doesn't already. This is a scripture-reading family.

Yet, the boys' names came to the parents with a surer sense of recognition than the girl's. Parents who had been raised as Latter-day Saints didn't need a concordance to identify Abraham and Isaac. A father who had performed as a child in the Hill Cumorah Pageant knew King Benjamin even if it took him a moment to remember the Old Testament Benjamin who was Joseph's brother. Yet, when Abigail's mother, thinking of the girl she hoped to have, first heard a still, small voice (the Holy Ghost? the child herself?) whisper *Abigail*, she didn't know the name was biblical.

How strange that the story of Abigail has slipped from our latter-day consciousness. I grew up knowing about Sarah, Rachel, and Hannah, Ruth the Gleaner, and the valiant Esther, but I didn't discover the bibilical Abigail until I began researching Puritan sermons in graduate school. My ignorance is not unique. When I presented my Gospel Doctrine class with a list of women in King David's time, everyone knew Bathsheba. Several remembered Michal. Only one or two, primed by my supplementary reading assignment, knew Abigail, a woman whose story is told in rich detail in 1 Samuel 25. That chapter was omitted from the Gospel Doctrine study guide this year. I decided to teach it anyway. There are so few fully developed female characters in the scriptures, I'm not willing to omit even one. Abigail is worth remembering.

Chapter 25 of 1 Samuel begins by introducing Nabal, a man wealthy in sheep and goats but "churlish and evil in his doing," and his wife Abigail, "a woman of good understanding, and of a beautiful countenance." Nabal's churlishness soon gets the family into deep trouble. When David, who is fleeing the wrath of Saul, sends for provisions, Nabal pretends not to know who he is, though his comment that "there be many servants nowadays that break away every man from his master" is probably an intentional slur on David's breech with his "master" Saul. Nabal is obviously a man who sees the world from the top down.

When David learns of Nabal's rebuke, he is so angry he tells his men to gird on their swords and prepare to take revenge on Nabal's house, at least the male portion of it: "So and more also do God unto the enemies of David, if I leave all that pertain to him by the morning light any that pisseth against the wall." The New English Bible cleans up the translation a bit: "God do the same to me and more if I leave him a single mother's son alive by morning!"

Enter Abigail. When a servant warns her of David's plan, she takes immediate action, loading up her asses with "two hundred loaves, and two bottles of wine ['two skins of wine' in The New English Bible], and five sheep ready dressed, and five measures of parched corn, and an hundred clusters of raisins, and two hundred cakes of figs." Intercepting David, Abigail prostrates herself on the ground and offers her gifts, compensating for her husband's ill manners by her own graciousness and generosity. (Lest anyone think of this as a particularly feminine mode of dealing with conflict, think of Jacob's reconciliation with Esau in Genesis 33.)

Nabal saw the world in hierarchical terms. As long as Saul was king, he was unwilling to support the outlaw David. Like many men foolishly loyal to superiors, Nabal treated his own subordinates with contempt. His servant was afraid to go to him with bad news "for he is such a son of Belial, that a man cannot speak to him." In contrast, Abigail was able to see through the outward trappings of earthly authority. When necessary, she called herself to an important duty, knowing better than to ask her churlish husband for permission. Like the prophet Samuel, she knew that "the Lord seeth not as man seeth" (1 Sam. 16:7). Like him, she also had the courage to instruct a king.

In her long speech to David (1 Sam. 25:24–31), she doesn't simply beg for mercy; she recalls him to a sense of his own mission, gently reminding him that he is not an ordinary warrior but a man with a destiny, a man who should be above petty revenge. Prophesying that he will live to rule Israel, she urges him to recognize his grievance with Nabal for the small thing it really is. (Here I really do like The New English translation better.)

> When the Lord has made good all his promises to you, and has made you ruler of Israel, there will be no reason why you should stumble or your courage falter because you have shed innocent blood or given way to your anger.

What is even more remarkable, Abigail's little sermon worked.

> And David said to Abigail, Blessed be the Lord God of Israel, which sent thee this day to meet me: And blessed be thy advice and blessed be thou, which has kept me this day from coming to shed blood, and from avenging myself with mine own hand.

I think of Abigail as an ancient-day Emma Lou Thayne or Valentina Inozemtseva, a woman sent to teach the world peace. Practical and visionary at the same time, she shared the abundance of her storehouse and her heart.

Abigail's story reminds us that the Bible is a potentially subversive document. No wonder kings and priests have always been afraid of letting the people read it, at least without proper guidance from those in charge. Samuel's books can be bent into a celebration of anointed power, but a reader has to ignore a lot to interpret them that way. David's unification of the kingdom at Jerusalem was a fleeting triumph, a fragile and momentary union of political and spiritual authority. He soon looked down from his palace onto Uriah's rooftop. One of my class members wondered if David's acceptance of Abigail's advice had as much to do with her beautiful face as her wise words. I prefer a less cynical interpretation. As long as David was dependent on God for his survival, he was able to listen as well as look.

I don't know if Abigail Carr's father has ever been asked if he named his daughter for Abigail Adams. I suspect not. Most people know as little about women in American history as about women in the Bible. However, it occurs to me that the eighteenth-century Abigail Adams had a lot in common with her Biblical predecessor. She was not shackled with a "churlish" husband, but she did have an absent one, and as a consequence, she had to deal with many of the emergencies of war on her own. She also had the capacity to understand the dangers of kingship. She had listened to her husband John and other patriots talk about the political relationship between the American colonies and Great Britain, and for one brief moment in 1776, she urged John to "Remember the Ladies." Like Samuel before her and Joseph Smith after, she reminded him of the dangers of unlimited power, "for all men would be tyrants if they could."

John laughed. He assured his wife that her female charms gave her all the power she needed. Despite his affection for Abigail, he was less willing to listen to her than to the Nabals around him: "We have been told that our Struggle has loosened the bands of Government everywhere. That Children and Apprentices were disobedient—that schools and Colleges were grown turbulent—that Indians slighted their Guardians and Negroes grew insolent to their Masters." John Adams preserved his revolution by denying its implications.

My little neighbor, Abigail Carr, was also born into a world of war and injustice. As she grows, may she be known for her good understanding as well as her beautiful countenance. May she treasure her name. May she too become a woman of peace.

DIALOGUE BY FAX:

JET LAG

Durham, New Hampshire
Sunday, 5:20 A.M.

I've been in Utah! Thank goodness my jet lag is over. Three days home I am awake once again with the birds, feeling chipper. My hair is curly, happy to be back in the eastern damp after a sojourn in the dry mountain air. I had a great time at the family reunion, but I'm glad to be back, glad to have negotiated once again the difficult geographical and psychic space between here and there.

Each time I fly west I retrace the path of the early Saints from the air—from New Hampshire over the finger lakes of New York, across Iowa and Nebraska into the Rockies. As the plane slows toward the Wasatch, I look down where my pioneer ancestors looked up. "This is the place!" I say to myself as the 747 glides over the lake toward the runway, the salt flats shimmering in the distance. My body can't catch up with my mind. By the time I catch my first glimpse of Mrs. Field's cookies, I've already put in an eight hour day, though the world doesn't know it. The clocks in the terminal say 10:10 A.M. though my stomach says noon.

I struggle with jet lag for at least two days, never sure when to eat and when to sleep, when to settle into the mountain securities of my childhood, when to resist the pull of space. Each morning, I awake on eastern time, surrounded by western blackness, listening hopelessly for birds.

You travel more than I, Emma Lou. How do you manage west to east and east to west, in body and spirit?

Salt Lake City, Utah
Monday, 11 A.M.

Jet lag has been a bear for me. My sleep originates in some circadian rhythms that haven't much to do with geography. I remember in Israel, still on Salt Lake time, I continued to wake at 4:30 A.M. So, not to wake Mel or our three then teenage daughters, I'd sit in the bathtub and write. I discovered something. I kept two journals, one for my purse to track places and facts, the other waiting for me at the hotel for the search to find what had really happened on that day in the Holy Land. One diary was the journey, the other the arrival. As the two became part of my book *Once in Israel*, I realized that one was prose and the other poetry. But coming home in that El Al 747 for eleven and one half hours, "rumpled as our sense of time . . . flying into the light . . . to live the daylight of March 24 three times," I wondered, "How many times have I wished for a day to do over? But now? In the timelessness of travel, being given the gift is to be robbed. Bound by the arms of our chairs, we go slack, hunchbacked, and wait with earphones for the movie, 'The Return of the Pink Panther,' to save us."

Time is precious only to our feel for it.

Durham, New Hampshire
Tuesday, 10 A.M.

I am fascinated by your image of hunchback travelers losing time as they gain it. Almost anything we want comes faster these days. We have instant noodles, instant money spilling from machines in airports, instant communications like this one, words becoming digital images and then pages in seconds. Then why does it feel like there's never enough time?

Mt. Hood, Oregon
Thursday, 4 P.M.

Maybe it's because in hurrying from place to place the psyche goes limp. What makes us think we can zoom from zone to zone without leaving streamers of ourselves trailing somewhere behind? So little time we allow for simply knowing where we are and who we are. Sometimes in the world of speed—including the Faxing of a letter to a friend—I long for the ruminating and the waiting that used to go into the writing and delivery of something like a love note, when a telegram was reserved for an emergency or exceptional celebration.

So much can seem impersonal in technology. Even checking

out at the grocery is hastened by dragging goods over an electronic recorder of selections and prices—so little exchange of much except money.

Durham, New Hampshire
Friday, noon

I know what you mean. I try to resist the notion that faster is better, yet I must admit I like my Fax machine. Maybe it's the combination of old and new, electronics and paper, that grabs me. There is something mysterious about a printed text emerging from a telephone—Gutenberg meeting Alexander Graham Bell! I love the incongruity, the craziness of it all.

Salt Lake City, Utah
Monday, 6 A.M.

Speaking of incongruity—yesterday I made my first trek to the Family History Center in the new Joseph Smith Memorial Building that used to be the "grande dame" Hotel Utah. My contact with ancestors had been one-to-one personal, never by way of lines on a genealogy chart. But my great-grandmother and namesake, Emma Turner, had found me in my dreams and I needed to find her. On the wall in what was Mother's room in our home hangs a sampler of hers, signed *Emma Turner, aged 7 years, September 8, 1840*. Embroidered by her are the alphabet, numbers to 14, and most dear:

> *When daily I kneel down to pray*
> *As I am taught to do,*
> *God does not care for what I say*
> *Unless I feel it too.*

Imagine—at seven! Who was she? What sort of woman did that seven-year-old become? You'd know, Laurel, with your historian's instincts and know-how. You could look at the old linen, the cross-stitches, and the colors of the thread and likely tell me about her literacy and home life, about what might compel her to become a Mormon, cross the ocean and the plains, be a first wife to my Great-grandfather Stayner.

Yesterday, with the marvel of a computer, under my still

uncertain commands, up came Emma Turner—ancestor file back to 1640, descendancy file ending with me. I had yet to input even my marriage forty-five years ago to Mel, our five daughters, their sturdy husbands, let alone eighteen grandchildren who will make lines into the twenty-first century. Talk about travel!

Durham, New Hampshire
Tuesday afternoon

Now you and I are traveling through time together. With Dawn's help, fragments of your past and mine are brought together in something like a book. As I read your poems and essays, I marvel at how different our journeys have been and how much the same. Does it matter that you've lived all your life in Salt Lake City and that I left the Rocky Mountains at twenty-two? Does it make a difference that you bore daughters, I a mixture of boys and girls? Does it matter that your family history placed you close to the center of the Church, and that I have lived all my adult life in what we used to call "the mission field"? Do our perspectives on life and Mormonism differ because you're seventy and I'm fifty-six, because I love libraries and you love tennis, because I get up early and you like to stay up late and sleep late? Does it matter that I am a scholar and you a poet? Like pages spilling out of forgotten pasts, our essays fill out our samplers and tell us who we were and where we've been.

Salt Lake City, Utah
Thursday night, 1 A.M.

What I realize seeing these essays is the speed of time. Was it only yesterday that I was surrounded by the "continuers" in my life—"Mother, Father, twelve uncles and my variegated aunts, even grandmas and their slow syllables on my unlighted spaces." I wrote those words more than a decade ago in *How Much for the Earth!* If it was true then, how much more now? My continuers are gone. At our table "mostly I am older than the rest. The house has thickened ... my husband and I, brothers, sisters, friends, startle ourselves with lingering past the childhood that no longer includes us."

78

Nor, now does it include our children in their childhood. But other children and their delight, our children's children of course, hover about our dailiness. Like the lines on the charts, I am intrinsically connected backward and forward, till everywhere now "is a dead and a living place." How lovely to be in on both. And how sheer the divider between here and there.

Durham, New Hampshire
Friday, 5 A.M.
Can anyone under fifty understand this strange mood we are in? Seeing my latest essays side by side with pieces written twenty years ago is like looking in a mirror and seeing a double image, the young mother I once was standing beside the grandmother I have become. The children who planted popsicle sticks on window sills in "Ode to Autumn" now have children of their own. Their science fiction novels have become high-tech careers in robotics, virtual reality, and computer-aided design. In their universe I am the wide-eyed toddler—or resistant teenager!

I too think about that strange doubleness compressed in Elijah's promise—turning my heart backward and forward, to progenitors and progeny. As my children have grown, the concept of "eternal increase" has taken on new meaning. It is not just the gift of children and grandchildren that stretches me across time, but the joy of entering another generation's imagined future. The five-month-old baby I wrote about in another essay in this book, that adorable child with "cushioned cheeks and pearled toes" is now a sophisticated college sophomore who dreams of living in Peru and who wonders whether the *Iliad* isn't a "guy's book."

I really get into this theme because it is a historian's topic. Our medium is time. Your medium in a way transcends time. You push boundaries through imagination, making the there here, and vice versa.

Salt Lake City, Utah
Thursday, midnight
How lucky that there are many ways of multiplying and replenishing. No matter our ages or marital status or demo-

graphics, part of us continues on by what we have to offer that has nothing to do with birthing or growing up and older. Like a sampler or a page in a diary or a reflection put into words.

Once I heard it said that it's easier to be a poet than a historian. The poet doesn't have to be hemmed in by facts! I'm not sure about that. I inherit the facts of my life from a mother who baked seven loaves of bread every other day in the city as expertly as she contended with occasional rattlesnakes at the cabin. She also got the giggles and taught us to hammer and saw and insisted on white gloves and a hat to exit our front door for any dash into the gentility she was born to. And never mind that two of her six brothers were General Authorities; she chose her meetings according to who in the family might be paying a visit and expect her at home for a chat and a piece of chocolate cake. Which of the facts of her life survive in me?

I discovered some by writing. Ironically, when she was dying of congestive heart failure at age seventy-six, the *Ensign*, not knowing, asked me to write a piece about mother-daughter relationships. Some assignment! Two days after her death, I sat in the big black leather rocker that had been my grandfather's and wrote "With Love, Mother." Now, twenty-two years later, my children grown, the essay could seem dated, but it's still resonant of what I felt that day and of what I learned from her, mostly about love. And history.

PROGENITORS

AND

PANCAKES

What better gift to each other than to share who we truly are, in all tones and with every kind of brush.

In the eternal family circle when we gather around the fire for family home evening on Monday nights in the celestial realm, will we be children of our parents or parents of our children?.

The greatest disservice we do each other is to give the constant appearance of "normalcy."

WITH LOVE, MOTHER

"As is the mother, so is her daughter." (Ezekiel 16:44)

WE WERE ALONE IN her room, my mother, Grace Richards Warner, and I, and she was dying. We both knew she was, but neither gave any indication of knowing. It would have clouded the assurance that each of us had always given the other—that things work out. That assurance of the goodness of life, of people, and of Heavenly Father was at the heart of our need now to comfort each other in the parting that loomed there like a thunderstorm, the kind of storm that Mother had prayed away when any of us were traveling and she was "working on the weather."

But now there was no staying the inevitable. That last day, the 23rd of December, 1972, had started like the others with a bath, a sponge bath of course, but a touching ritual that had lent us a closeness long lost in the routine of adulthood. Just before Thanksgiving Mother had suffered a massive heart attack. After three weeks of intense hospital care, it had become apparent that the damaged heart would never be able to pump the fluid from her lungs and she would die, maybe in a day, maybe in a.... No one really knew. So we brought her home to the rooms she loved in the home she had built with us fifteen years before when my father died at fifty-nine.

Our house had become hers, our lives and those of our five daughters a running, hectic, noisy, and very alive part of her dailiness. Until the day she went to the hospital, she had been a vital, perky, busy participant in our lives and in those of scores of family and friends who now came to her with a terrible need to hold on to her.

It was that need that eased my hand with the washcloth across her shoulders and down her arms. Bathing her was somehow a return to the essentials of human contact. She was tiny—only 4 feet 10 inches—barely to the neckties of my father and husky brothers and husband. Her body was like a baby's: soft, plump, white, smooth, and without a blemish. I laughed as I washed her feet and rubbed fresh smelling powder on her back, telling her, "You're marvelous, Mother. You take me back to bathing my babies—to all that delight in making them sweet and clean."

And I'd pat her and smooth her nightie and make sure her pillow was fluffed just right against her cheek. She'd smile too—even that day—and take my hand covered in powder and lotion and grip it thumb to thumb, letting me feel her affirmation flood into my palm and up my arm and into my soul. If ever there were a bond between mother and daughter, it was there in that bath time, growing firm and tight for anything that might come.

In the days since, I've thought often of how that all worked as I've looked at my own girls and pondered the reasons for good and not-so-good times together. It seems that a lot of having what psychologists call "a great mother-daughter relationship" is dependent upon my being able to maintain the kind of warm, obvious, gentle concern for them that I exhibited when they were babies and I had the joyful job of bathing them.

This may appear ridiculous. How can a mother sustain that feeling of active guardianship throughout the life of her growing, independent, challenging daughters? How can she continue to demonstrate in concrete ways that she still cherishes them? Surely the actual process of washing and anointing with love is long gone, as is the need for that kind of authentic motherliness. But between any one of my daughters and me there is a tremendous need to explore and keep alive on a very daily basis those elements that made that early association so satisfying for both of us.

I do think it's possible, and here's how it might go: It involves all of the miracle of being human and demands a constant sharing between me as a mother and each of my daughters in all five areas of human potential—the physical, the emotional, the mental, the social, and the spiritual.

First, the physical. How easy it is to forget the power of

touch in our relationships with a child. I remember when each of my girls was tiny how I couldn't hug her tight enough or rock her long enough or soothe her softly enough. What makes me think that same touch has lost its magic for either of us? True, a lot of it is not feasible now; but I can still pat her shoulder when she looks as if she needs it or squeeze her when she's glad or sad. And what better than a good night kiss to seal the day with I love you?

And there's another side to the physical. I played and worked with her when she was little. Snowmen and mud pies and jumping in the pool we did together. Now we can throw a party or hit a ball or ski a mountain or pull weeds and share the same exhilaration we did then. It all tightens the bond. It was this same touching tenderness that made my mother my best nurse and most eager companion on many an excursion; she never forgot to express her love by hand.

Then there's the emotional. When my daughter was small I was in on her every hurt or excitement. When she came running to me while I was gardening, saying, "Mommy, butterflies scare me," I held her and smiled the fear away. What difference should it make if now she's afraid of going to a new school or of breaking up with that special boy or of the awesomeness of thinking about marriage? And if the sharing of traumas draws me closer to her, why shouldn't I tell her about mine and allow her the privilege of smiling me out of them—or at least of hearing them and understanding me better?

Someone once said that the greatest disservice we do each other is to give the constant appearance of "normalcy." No one is free of weakness, failure, ineptitude, anxiety. To participate in the emotional life of my girl, I must be willing to accept her problems without condemnation and to share mine without fear of losing my status of the all-knowing, all-powerful, always-in-control grown-up. It is her humanness and ability to feel, to laugh, to cry, that draw me to her. Why not let that communion work actively for both of us?

And why not preserve one of our greatest outlets for tension—laughter? Always we've laughed. I remember getting the giggles during a violin recital when she was ten and chuckling at the antics of the puppy or at the embarrassment of my falling flat on the ice in a group of strangers. What pleasant, binding exchange can we now have in simply laughing together? In trading stories of the day or breaking up over the crazy happenings in a wild household just before a party?

In the sharing of frailty and laughter my mother was always there to listen, to tell, and to laugh—almost more and more as the years drew us both into womanhood and its complexities. And more and more her understanding drew me to her for the intimacy of sharing grief and joy.

Now what about the mental? When my daughter was a child I loved to teach her, to learn with her—how to draw a monkey, how to put the visible man together, what words were, why the sun came up. And now that she's a "people," there are horizons neither of us has explored. What finer grain for my mental mill than her saying, "Read this, Mother. You'll like it. And I want to talk to you about it."

Am I disqualified, because we are now one adult to another, from reading what she's written—a paper or report—and gleaning as well as constructively criticizing? By sharing the intellectual—books, concerts, plays, art, ideas—we cultivate awareness not only of our world but of each other and our responses to that world. In consensus or divergence, we can foster vast areas of interest that will pull us together for talk and stimulation. Mother never lost interest in life or in me and was always my severest and most sought-after critic—of what I thought, what I saw, what I believed, what I wrote. I needed her.

And about the social. When she was young, my little girl and I went everywhere together. She absorbed my feelings for people in the grocery store, at meetings, in the houses around the block. Then when she went on her own, a birthday party, a Primary class, a bike ride were subject to detailed and exuberant accounting. We shared it all. And in depth. How more likely then to indicate my continued cherishing of her than to care—really care—about all that: about who said what to whom at school, about why she's jumping when the phone rings tonight, about the possible disaster of going or not going to that out-of-town formal.

And what insight might she have into adult workings if I mention the crisis in that class I taught today, or the funny situation at the party last night, or the poignant struggle of that friend in trouble this afternoon? How better to meet our need to confide than to give each other current specifics from our lives and refuse to float apart on inch-deep generalities?

In another social way, we have the beautiful right to lend to each other's lives the people who occupy ours. In my mother's death I realized more than ever how she had exercised this right. Her friends are mine because she made me feel an important part of her life with them. In the same way she made my friends hers. One of my oldest friends said not long ago, "One reason I always liked to come to your house was that I never felt that I was just your friend. I felt like your parents and your brothers all thought of me as their friend too—and that made me more welcome than anything." What more *expansive* gift is there than my daughter's sharing her friends—boys and girls—to broaden my base? And what better can I share with her than genuine companions from my sphere who will care about and coddle her into and through adulthood as my mother's friends did me? What range, what diversity, what depth we can hand to each other through the people that we love!

Finally, there is the spiritual. When my little girl wondered about crocuses in the spring or the taste of snow or the speed of a hummingbird outside the cabin, I relished the chance to marvel with her at the glory and the Giver. Throughout the day, by the bed and at the table, we shared every prayer of gratitude and supplication. My feelings about divinity and grace were hers through telling and example. I made sure she knew of my profound need for strength beyond myself, and of my easy faith that it was there. Almost by osmosis she sensed and enjoyed the rites and privileges of believing.

What makes me suppose that such osmosis is not still occurring as we tell each other what we feel about our spiritual soundings? Can she tell me how she felt about that talk or someone's seeming hypocrisy or someone else's fine sensitivity? Can we talk about what Jesus might have done in a touchy situation that confronts me? Can she share a Sunday School lesson at the table or expect my during-the-day prayers to be for her when a big test is in the offing? Do we have access to each other's spiritual makeup so that it is as real and operative in bringing us together as fixing a meal in the same kitchen might be?

On that last day, my mother's hand in mine, I knew a feeling for continuity and faith as I never had. Through her lifetime of "working on the weather," of praying us through crises, of showing us how to give—goods, time, interest, ourselves—of demonstrating a caring, laughing, loving, expectant way to go, Mother had done it all. She had preserved believing and had led us quietly and happily in the paths of righteousness by making those paths flower with fun and good spirit and camaraderie. Storms had been met with the certainty that they would pass and that like Job, where we could not control our circumstances, we could control our responses.

So now I was losing her, my *Grace*, my pillar, my soft, soft lady with the lamp. I leaned close to her, concerned that she hear, as she always had, my concern. I'd been a daughter different by far from the one I'd always imagined her wanting—a needlepoint, demure daughter more like her than like my athletic, involved father. We'd joked about it before, but now I said, "Mother, I know you've always wished I'd take a gentler horse."

She opened her brown eyes, flashing in dark circled settings, squeezed my hand harder, and said, "No. I always loved you on the wild one."

And there it was. The whole secret of why she succeeded as a mother and why the bond of that moment held us firm. In every way she treasured me—physically, emotionally, mentally, socially, spiritually. She loved me as a person, as a unique, functioning, floundering potential, as truly a child of God. In spite of my failings, my impetuousness, my differences from her, our differences over the years, she loved me. And she showed it, always. She loved me as an adult just as she did when I was a little girl. She knew how to let her love mature and take on the dimension of whatever stage we both were in. And along the way she let me go, gave me the honor of being myself, knowing that that was the surest way to bring me back.

That night just before Christmas I had to let her go. While smiling at some flowers that had just arrived, Mother gasped and was gone. Alert and wise to the end, she remained my link with how to do it. And I'll keep going back and back to that memory for constant help in trying to see that my five girls grow up as I did—with love, Mother.

A PIONEER IS NOT A WOMAN WHO MAKES HER OWN SOAP

I SUPPOSE EVERY MORMON woman has measured herself at one time or another against "the pioneers." Am I as stalwart? As self-reliant? As devoted to the gospel? As willing to sacrifice? Could I crush my best china to add glitter to a temple, bid loving farewell to a missionary husband as I lay in a wagon bed with fever and chills, leave all that I possessed and walk across the plains to an arid wilderness?

For me, such thoughts have a way of recurring at awkward moments. Perhaps my full pedigree of handcart-pushing, homesteading grandmothers is the cause, but I remember being wheeled into a delivery room on one occasion, surrounded by sterile sheets, rubber-gloved nurses, and the most sophisticated of fetal-monitoring equipment, and saying to the doctor: "I never would have made a pioneer!"

Fortunately for my ego, he laughed and answered: "Of course you would have. You would have done all right in a field."

I am sure he was right. Given no other option, I could have given birth, as my own Grandmother Thatcher did, in a log cabin while recovering from smallpox. Heroism often consists in simply surviving under tough odds. Yet books of remembrance seldom record the pain, and even less frequently the petty complaints, quarrels, and insecurities that so often accompany great deeds. That is why I enjoy a passage from the journal of Henrietta E. Williams, in which she described an ordinary but trying day when the pioneers had stopped to shoe cattle and reset wagon tires.

> They knew that I was no cook, but left that job for me. I built a fire after gathering buffalo chips, and getting it started, the wind playing with it as it pleased. I put the dutch oven on to heat with the cover by the side of it. I made a pie of dried apples, putting it into

the oven, the lid still heating, and turned toward the wagon several
yards away from the fire for safety. A nice cow sneaked up and
helped herself to the pie and sneaked off, when a girl called me to
look at my rice. I had a hard time cooking the biscuits as I was
jumping in and out of the wagon, climbing over the provision box,
watching my baby girl and getting what [my husband] wanted as
it was his misfortune never to find anything he was looking for. The
fire had its own way of burning. I thought, "Oh, Zion, will we ever
reach thee?"[1]

As a modern woman, whose moments of trial often come at
suppertime, I take comfort in this homely anecdote. I hope as
journal keepers we will share with our descendants our times of
discouragement as well as the moments we want to preserve in
bronze. I also hope that we will remember that the pioneers
were people too.

"Oh, Zion, will we ever reach thee?" Since Zion is the
"pure in heart" as the Doctrine and Covenants tells us, all of us
live most of our lives on the trail. We are still pioneers. I suppose most Latter-day Saints recognize that. Our challenges are
just as important as those of the past. Our testing is as crucial;
our contributions may be as great. But it is difficult sometimes
to recognize just what those challenges really are, and sometimes the example of the pioneers seems to get in the way.

Recently I heard an announcement in our ward urging couples to participate in a temple excursion. The motivational
device that the speaker used was a familiar one: "Of course, it is
a little inconvenient to ride on a bus all night and do endow-
ments all day, but when you compare an air-conditioned bus
with the covered wagons the pioneers had, you can see that
our sacrifices are pretty small."

But eternal progression cannot be measured in miles, or by
the false equation: the more bumps and the more lost sleep,
the more valiant the Saint. No. Despite air-conditioning and
padded seats, our sacrifices *are* often as great, and our challenges *are* as profound as any in the past.

I have a friend who says that the equivalent of crossing the
plains in her life is driving to Primary each week through Boston

rush-hour traffic. I have another who sees a contemporary version of facing social ostracism in taking four children under five to the playground in the university apartment complex where she and her husband live. Having faced both of these trials, I am not ready to dismiss them as trivial. Urban congestion and zero population growth are as real to many Latter-day Saints as sagebrush and mobs were to their progenitors.

But there are other dimensions to our pioneering. We have usually thought of the "frontier" as an empty place beyond white settlement, a desert or prairie to be cultivated and civilized. But in recent years, scholars of Indian-white relations have suggested another definition. A frontier is not a geographical space but a social space, an environment in which two different cultures meet and interact. In this sense, Latter-day Saints today are at the pushing edge of a new frontier.

A hundred years ago, Church members gathered to a Zion which was perceived as a geographically unified and economically cohesive community of Saints. An adobe brick meetinghouse and a Zion's cooperative Mercantile Institution on the same street of the same town symbolized a unity of secular and spiritual life. Because there was no distinction between one's ward and one's neighborhood, my great-grandmother could borrow yeast and gather spiritual strength from the same group of women.

How different my own life! I am a citizen of a New Hampshire town of 10,000 people in which fewer than two dozen, including infants, are Latter-day Saints. I owe allegiance to a Mormon ward which meets in a city fifteen miles away and draws members from twenty towns in two states. Thus, at the interface of these two cultures, I experience a different frontier than my great-grandmother.

Yet the ideals of community life and responsibility which the early Saints carried with them to the Great Basin are still greatly needed in my world. As a granddaughter of pioneers, I know that my town and my ward both matter, that Heavenly Father has given me a stewardship in each, and that only by bringing the two together on the frontier of my daily life can I ever hope to reach "Zion."

92

Frontiers can be disordered and even chaotic places where men and women appear at their worst as well as their best. Yet an essential quality of the first pioneers was optimism, an ability to see new possibilities in a strange and unsettling environment. To beautify the desert, they needed faith in God, but they also needed faith in themselves and in their ability to help shape the world. The need for that faith has not diminished.

Women have been preservers of continuity from generation to generation. I cherish that role. I like to collect old furniture, can fruit, tie quilts, and grind whole wheat. It is important to preserve the skills of the past, but in any generation that is not enough. In passing along our own spiritual heritage, we must be pioneers.

"Let us not narrow ourselves up," Brigham Young cautioned our great-grandfathers and grandmothers. "We must lengthen our stride," another Prophet has urged us. A pioneer is not a woman who makes her own soap. She is one who takes up her burdens and walks toward the future. With vision and with courage she makes the desert bloom.

Note

[1] Nancy Clement Williams, *After One Hundred Years*, (Independence, Mo.: Zion's Printing and Publishing Co., 1951), p. 157.

CHIAROSCURO

IN ART THERE IS A technique that uses dark shades of different tones to heighten the effect of light. Rembrandt and Shakespeare used it—in paintings, in plays. Juxtaposed with or superimposed on darkness, light becomes more radiant than it might have been by itself. This technique affects more than contrast; it allows the light to surge from within as if imbued with ethereal properties that transcend ordinary conceptions of warmth or brilliance. The technique is called chiaroscuro: *chiaro,* light; *oscuro,* dark. Chiaroscuro. The word itself comes luminous edged in gray.

What in life does not come edged in dark? Out of the dark burst most of our moments with light—a baby born, a storm over, health recovered, a quarrel resolved, believing restored. Yet among us, especially as Mormons, there is a diffidence, a pale reluctance to deal with the dark that preceded the birth, the clearing, the getting well, the loving, the faith. The charcoal of our unsettling thoughts or feelings is painted out by the fear of appearing faithless or inept or not in tune with the gospel.

Too often what we know about each other, certainly too much of what we read in Church publications, histories, manuals, hear from pulpits, will never be as rich as it might be until we somehow learn to allow, on paper as well as in talk, the getting acquainted with both the yellows and the grey-browns in ourselves and each other.

A few years ago I stood by the bedside of my Aunt Evalyn Richards who was dying of cancer. She would have been ninety in a month. Ever since I was a little girl she had pampered me with attention and gifts, not the least of which was the privilege of getting to see her during these last years of her life when she became a virtual recluse, almost blind, and deaf enough that her conversations were always sustained at a glass-shattering pitch. She'd had only one child of her own, a boy born with club feet, who died at twenty-one, and she and Uncle Willard had taken on my brothers and me to pamper and sustain in brave and unfailing ways.

That Sunday morning my brother Rick and I left the still elegance of her home silenced by a strange inertia. He had given her a blessing, I had held her too slim, for the first time unmanicured hand, and we both had tried to sift into her sleeping some notion of how we loved her. But we were confounded by mammoth intrusions into our sense of things: In Aunt Evalyn's dying we would become the "older generation." Not only would we have the concern and obligation of putting together her funeral, virtually the last ever to be for those wondrously impossible aunts and uncles, mother and father, but we would have to know enough to do it—to arrange for the funeral, and assume the rights, duties, honors and fears of being the ones in charge, not only of it, but of life.

In my efforts to assume both responsibilities, I discovered a truth I now must grapple with. I realized how little we knew about Aunt Evalyn. Oh, she was at family parties, she and Uncle Willard came to our home for Christmas for forty years, and they lived in a cabin in Mt. Air just one straight stretch away from where we lighted our lamps from the generator Uncle Willard concocted between the stream and their front porch. The pony we rode was their son's, the horseshoe pit, theirs, and Aunt Evalyn invited us in for hot cross buns with lots of raisins, and birthday parties on Valentine's Day. Though we never heard her, we knew she played the violin as a girl, had studied in Paris. And over the years she had given me things like a play store and "traveling towels" to pack for the trips I never took until college. She had bestowed outrageously generous gifts on all of our children as they grew up, for Christmases, marriages, births. And once a month or so we'd had visits at her house about the usual happenings of a big family. But as Rick and I tried to put together with another cousin even an obituary, we realized in the kind of panic that attends having missed the last train, that Aunt Evalyn was gone, and that with her were gone the memories, the details, the light and shadow of a lifetime that would never be remembered.

I urgently wanted to ask her on that Sunday, "Aunt Evalyn, why did you leave the Church? What happened to you when you were abandoned by the boy you adopted? Did it help to move when Little Willard died? Did you want the blessing Rick gave you at the last? Why did you refuse to play your violin?" and more than anything, "Aunt Evalyn, who did you look to all those years that you were the older generation? Is this aloneness what I will feel for the rest of my life?"

I wish I had known her depths and heights, painted in rich chiaroscuro. I wish I had known her—and she me. A different kind of love would have prevailed, an informed, informative love. What might we have lent to each other's grappling with any coming of age? Maybe new seeing and believing and being able.

I long to talk with my two so-alike and so-different grandmothers Warner and Richards. I expect to in a life to come. But I want to have a chance here and now to be real for my children and grandchildren, to give us the mutual exchange that can teach and empower our lives by knowing what we feel and understand and believe.

It is not always easy. It takes real talking together. But what better gift to each other than to know who we truly are, in all tones and with every kind of brush? Surely Aunt Evalyn had her lights and darks. Who has not been wrenched by loss and anger? Who has not wrestled with decisions and been filled with remorse over a wrong one (even in something as un-earth-shattering as a diet)? What makes me think it's not the blows as much as the triumphs that have shaped my strengths or anyone else's? And whoever has not had strengths fade in the face of temptation or fear, each of us, so vulnerable, so unique, yet so remarkable in our ability to rebound and rebuild. Give me the relationship that can muster for the dark as well as for the light. And I'll be in on love that is real and deep and lasting. With chiaroscuro playing like sun in and out of clouds on the weather of our trying, like everyone else, to manage, for heaven's sake, what's there.

FIRST LOSS

My grandma shared her bed with me,
Till she died when I was twelve.
We slept with breaths that matched.
(I went to sleep every night restraining
Deliberately one extra breath in five
To let her slower time teach mine to wait.)

She never knew I waited, but talked
To me of Mendon where Indians ferreted
Her isolated young-wife home for cheese and honey,
And of Santa Barbara and eerie tides that
Drew her now for gentle months away from snow,
And sometimes of Evangeline lost in the forest
primeval.

Grandma's batter-beating, white-gloved, laughing
Daytime self slept somewhere else, and she visited
Mellifluous beyond my ardent reach, always off
Before me. I followed into rhythms I knew
Were good, her chamois softness weighing me
By morning toward a cozy common center.

She died there, when I was twelve.
I was sleeping, alien, down the hall
In a harder bed, isolated from the delicate
Destruction that took its year to take her.
That night my mother barely touched my hair
And in stiff, safe mechanics twirled the customary

Corners of my pillow one by one. "Grandma's gone,"
She said. Crepuscular against the only light
Alive behind her in the hall, she somehow left.
My covers fell like lonely lead on only me.
I lay as if in children's banks of white where
After new snow we plopped to stretch and carve

Our shapes like paper dolls along a fold.
Now, lying on my back, I ran my longest arms
From hip to head, slow arcs on icy sheets,
And whispered childhood's chant to the breathless
room:
>"Angel, Angel, snowy Angel,
>"Spread your wings and fly."

A LITTLE BIT OF HEAVEN

MY GRANDPA THATCHER TOLD two kinds of stories—real life tales of the Old West and Bible stories. I sat politely through the latter so as not to hurt his feelings, but what I really wanted to hear when I pulled a hassock to his knee was how he almost drowned in the mill race when he was three, how he got caught once filling his pant legs with candy from the old ZCMI in Logan, how he baited his hook with squirrel tails and caught more fish than his horse could carry, how he survived a snow storm while tending sheep above Gentile Valley, how he got away from the U.S. Marshall on his twenty-first birthday and voted despite the anti-polygamy laws. To my mind, it was Grandpa's life that had the wonder and rightness of scripture.

Once in awhile, despite all my cousin and I could do, Grandpa would switch to the Bible. He would begin with a story from the Old Testament or a parable, then he would grow intense, plant a gnarled hand on one of our knees, and looking intently through the spiraling circles of his thick glasses, begin to quote whole passages from memory. Cataracts had left him nearly blind. He could just make out the day's headlines with the magnifying glass he kept on the radio beside his chair. Unable to read the scriptures any longer, he would call up whole pages memorized fifty or sixty years before. I was convinced he knew all four standard works by heart. I can still hear him reciting Malachi:

> But who may abide the day of his coming? and who shall stand when he appeareth? for he is like a refiner's fire, and like fuller's soap.

I felt scalded but somehow cleansed by those words. Even now I think of Grandpa first and Handel second when I hear that passage. I'm still not sure what fuller's soap is, but as a child I knew it had something to do with the way the veins stood out high and dark on Grandpa's mottled hands.

I disagreed with Grandpa but once. That was a day he ended his scriptural excursion with a description of heaven. "The whole earth will be resurrected and will become as a sea of glass," he said. I don't remember the exact words. He may have quoted from Revelation or from section 130 of the Doctrine & Covenants, but I will never forget the effect of the image. "But I wouldn't want to live on a sea of glass," I said firmly. Grandpa looked surprised and a little amused. "It will be beautiful. Like crystal. We will have everything we want; all we will have to do is pluck nourishment from the air." That did it. Here was a man who at ninety still relished "a little vinegar gravy" with his fish and wanted his stewing hens "good and fat" talking about plucking his nourishment from the air. I could see there was no point in arguing, but I had no intention of going to such a slick and glassy hereafter.

His "sea of glass" has come to mean something quite different to me now, but the skepticism I felt at Grandpa's knee has not left me. The scriptures tell us so little about the hereafter and what they tell us is so often figurative, that it seems futile to draw hard conclusions. I believe there *is* a heaven and I have faith that the best things in human experience foreshadow it, but beyond that I'm not willing to go. I am often surprised at the convictions of others. Not too long ago, I heard an earnest young sister stand in testimony meeting and say that she couldn't let another week go by knowing that her husband, the ward clerk, was writing down the names of those who had spoken and that her name was missing. "When I come to the day of judgment and Christ opens that record and asks why five months went by without my bearing my testimony, I won't know what to say." It must be comforting to ward clerks, whose job is tedious and often thankless, to believe that their minutes will survive the refiner's fire and the fuller's soap to be shelved in the heavens. But it's not very comforting to me. My testimonies are usually silent ones. I always thought they'd been heard.

Then take the matter of the eternal family circle. When we gather around the fire for family home evening on Monday nights in the celestial realm, will we be children of our parents or parents of our children? If both, won't that circle continue in an unbroken spiral from Adam to the last child of the millennium and thus cease to be a "family" in the private and exclusive sense? "Brother" and "Sister" will be more meaningful titles in such a setting than either "parent" or "child." It is easy to be sentimental about Mormon theology. Starry-eyed young parents look down on their newly blessed babe and want that precious relationship to continue forever. Grandparents look at a family portrait taken on their Golden Wedding anniversary and project the cherished image into the hereafter. I hope that at least some of these hopes are realized. I would like to be with Grandpa again, yet if I am ever ushered into the celestial kingdom, I'm not sure I'll be able to find him. In heaven he will not be a gnarled old man, nor will I be a little girl. As two adults, what will we say to each other on that sea of glass?

A friend of mine thinks the celestial kingdom will be largely devoted to reproduction. The husband and wife relationship will endure, as the scriptures say, and it will be polygamous. This is because one wife will not be sufficient to people the new earth which each exalted male priesthood bearer will inherit. "Reproduction will take place just as it does on this earth," she says quite calmly. "Therefore, there is no other way." I admire her composure, especially since she is happily and monogamously married and has no intention of adding to her merely middle sized Mormon family. I know a lot of people who share her view, translating "eternal increase" in the celestial sphere quite literally. They may be right, yet if like begets like why does one need an exalted *physical* body to give birth to spirits? It's a puzzle.

The story is told of Charles Eliot Norton, renowned Harvard medievalist, who approached the pearly gates only to recoil in horror: "How gauche, how overdone, how Renaissance!" Each of us envisions heaven according to our own dreams.

As we were driving along the capital beltway after our tour of the Washington Temple, I asked my husband and children how they pictured the celestial kingdom. My second son said he didn't know, but he hoped it had a library. My husband said he thought it would be much like this life; he didn't think there would be any sitting around and he planned on doing some engineering. My oldest son said he hoped it looked like the White Mountains of New Hampshire. Our daughter, who had looked closely at the floral arrangements at the temple, said she hoped all the flowers would be real. Somebody else said they thought heaven was a place where you could have a ten-speed bike without a padlock. I suppose few ordinary mortals are capable of imagining the divine. Most of us furnish our dreams of heaven with treasures laid up on earth.

I can understand how the pioneers of Utah could banish Adam and Eve into a world of sagebrush and endless sky, picturing the plan of salvation as it unfolds in the Salt Lake Temple as a progression from a wild and terrifying natural environment to an increasingly refined, sheltered, and luxuriously chandeliered heaven. The new temples are more efficient than the old, having departed from the pioneer floor plan in order to process more names, yet they still cling to that frontier image of heaven, a symbolic environment which has less meaning in a day when every suburban shopping center sells velvet cushions. I am waiting for the Church architect to implement section 130. Glass is at least as scriptural as marble. The celestial room of the Washington Temple, for example, might have opened into the tops of the trees with wide vistas of woods and sky. Rain and snow and changing seasons would have been no problem. The Mormon universe is not static.

As an apprentice historian I sometimes wonder about my own future in a realm of "glass and fire, where all things for their glory are manifest, past, present, and future," but I can't help hoping. The prophet tells us that:

> This earth, in its sanctified and immortal state, will be made like unto crystal and will be a Urim and Thummim to the inhabitants who dwell thereon, whereby all things pertaining to an inferior kingdom, or all kingdoms of a lower order, will be manifest to those who dwell on it. (D&C 130:7)

Grandpa's sea of glass may be a Gypsy ball or a heavenly video screen revealing without effort all that has been and all that will be. But then again, it may be more like his magnifying glass, a simple tool for enlarging the vision of the one who holds it. The Urim and Thummim metaphor is enticing, for on earth its powers were available only when the prophet exerted his own. Perhaps that heavenly crystal is only a larger historical perspective, giving us the distance between ourselves and our own experience which will allow us to give it form and meaning. I hope so. If in heaven I can come to know and love Grandpa in childhood, in maturity, and in age, that will be reward enough.

DANISH PANCAKES

NOT SO LONG AGO, one of my students asked if the Mormons were that group out in Utah who had a big vault in the mountain where they kept dead bodies. Genealogy seems to have replaced polygamy as the great Mormon mystery.

I admit to mixed feelings on the topic. Sometimes I envy new members of the Church who can begin their research with themselves, moving back through the generations in the happy sense that they got there first. My friend Nancy Bussey glows when she comes home from a research trip to Nova Scotia. Often she has a new name or date to enter in her book, and sometimes there are completed records to take to the temple. It is a very different process for those of us whose great- and sometimes great-great-grandparents did their own temple work. As for pushing the pedigree back to Adam, ardent genealogists on six sides have either traced our lines to mysterious progenitors like Morgan of Glynfwl or struck a dead end somewhere in 1770 in New Jersey.

I know it is slothful to say that one's genealogy has "been done." There are all those collateral lines nobody thought about and all those mistakes to be discovered and corrected. That's just the trouble. New members of the Church can pursue their pedigrees, happy in the knowledge they are the first pickers in the orchard. The rest of us are left to crawl around on our hands and knees looking for drops. Unless, of course, we define genealogy as something more than bagging names.

A couple of years ago I decided to go through my "genealogy drawer," a catch-all for fading library notes, unlabeled photographs, and miscellaneous family histories collected from more dutiful relatives. My sister Layle, who has no more time for such things than I, had conscientiously verified and retyped our family's four-generation pedigree and family records, as the Church had asked us to do. As I thought about putting her crisp, clean sheets into my flat *Book of Remembrance*, I felt a nudge of guilt. She had done her part in making the old records accessible to the next generation. Surely I could do something too.

For several Sunday afternoons I read and sorted. I was surprised, though I shouldn't have been, at how male-centered the collection really was. There were stories about Robert Siddoway's conversion, about Jeppe Folkman's imprisonment for preaching the gospel, about Henry Harries' abandonment of his father's mills to follow the Saints, but almost nothing about Emma Jackson or Serena Anderson or Mary Rees. True, there were intriguing anecdotes about Alley Kitchen in one of the Hezekiah Thatcher family newsletters, but the same unconscious bias that gave his name to the family organization set the tone for the resulting histories.

Notice how on a traditional pedigree chart the eye scans upward along male lines. The maternal progenitors are there, but shifting surnames makes it difficult to retain a sense of continuity from generation to generation. Even more difficult to grasp are the links between mothers and sons or fathers and daughters. Accomplished genealogists are wonderfully adept at making the connections, but for the rest of us it is easier to single out a branch than to comprehend the tree.

I decided to start by rearranging what I had. I found pictures of myself, my mother, my grandmother, and my great-grandmother all taken at about the same age. Lining them up on a Book of Remembrance-sized sheet, I typed place of birth, age at marriage, and number of children under each, then labeled the composition, "My Mother's Mother's Mother's Mother." The comparative dresses (and noses) were revealing. So were the numbers. To my surprise, I had the second-largest family (after my great-grandmother who was married at nineteen and had fourteen children). I was also interested to discover that only my mother had stayed in the state of her birth. From Wales to Utah to Idaho to Massachusetts there had been a continuing pattern of migration. I was both more and less deviant than I thought.

Next I made a conscious effort to move beyond familiar names. After spending a Sunday afternoon poring over Preston

Parkinson's wonderful book (*The Utah Woolley Family*), I no longer thought of myself as a Thatcher from the hills of West Virginia. I had become a Pennsylvania Quaker. That was twice satisfying. I could now feel that my son had strengthened rather than weakened family tradition by going to school in Philadelphia. (His parents and siblings had gone to Boston.) I could also rejoice that long before the Church was organized some of my female progenitors had belonged to a group who offered women equality.

My next project was to think about ethnicity. My own students have made me aware that in some New England towns it really matters whether one is Irish, Italian, or French Catholic. I wondered if all local color had been washed out in the Mormon migration. I divided a circle into sixteen segments, one for each of my own and my husband's great-grandparents, then looked at place of birth. Now when my youngest daughter asked me, "What am I?" I could respond: "You are 1/4 German, 1/4 English, 1/8 Welsh, 1/16 Danish, 1/16 Norwegian, 1/16 West Virginian, and 3/16 Pennsylvanian." A melting pot indeed, but one with a decidedly northern European flavor.

That got me to thinking about food. Might it be possible to trace female inheritance through recipes? I thought about the Danish pancakes my Grandmother Thatcher used to make, huge dinner-plate-sized crepes, fried in butter, then filled with stewed gooseberries, warm from the pan, a bulging pocket of buttery tartness as satisfying and astringent as any of Grandpa's stories. (I make them still, substituting rhubarb because gooseberries, which carry a white pine blight, cannot be legally grown in New Hampshire.)

As I contemplated those pancakes, I had a distressing thought. Grandma Thatcher's *father* was Danish, her mother was *Norwegian*. Was the family recipe I cherished another relic of patriarchal power? So much for my sense of cultural continuity. A few months later, I was in Utah. Visiting with my Aunt Fleda, I remembered the pancakes.

"How is it," I asked, "that Grandma Thatcher made *Danish* rather than Norwegian pancakes, since her mother was

Norwegian?"

Aunt Fleda seemed more amused than puzzled by the question. "I don't know," she said. "We always called them Danish pancakes."

"Well, did she make any other traditional dishes?" I asked.

"Oh, yes," Uncle Alf interjected. "She made great Danish dumplings."

"With potato," Aunt Fleda finished. Then she added, "But I think she got that recipe from Sister Larsen who lived in the house behind us in Logan."

I instantly knew what was wrong with my question. Here I was trying to compress family history to the width of a pedigree chart. After all, I didn't learn how to make Danish pancakes from my mother, who doesn't even like them, but from my paternal aunt. My grandmother could have done so, too. Just as likely, she picked up her ethnic recipes from her next-door neighbor. I fully suspect, though I resist admitting it, that my Grandmother Siddoway did the same. I like to think of her mustard pickles (which I also make) as an inheritance of her Welsh mother or her English mother-in-law, but probably they came from some Relief Society dinner in Teton City, Idaho.

Family history is remade in each generation, which is why genealogy, like housework, is never done. I am thinking of another family recipe, a wonderfully pink soup made with strained rhubarb, sweetened and thickened with cornstarch. I got the recipe from *Sunset* magazine when we lived in California a number of years ago. Only after it had become a springtime perennial at our house did I learn that my Grandma Thatcher had also made it. She didn't call it "Rabarbergrod," as the magazine did, or even "Danish Dessert," though it bears a faint resemblance to the packaged variety. She called it "Barn Paint." By that name the recipe will be passed down (or lost) to my children's children's children.

Laurel Thatcher Ulrich • 1975

THOUGHTS FOR THE GOLDEN WEDDING

Scallop-toothed in third grade,
Thatcher carries his grandfather's name,
And the genetic calendar
That programs twelve-year molars at sixteen.
The white kernel that popped from his mouth at dinner
   Wednesday,
Leaving blood on the cob,
Left him smiling Sylvia Alsop's smile,
Though only a Thatcher from Gentile Valley would know why.

Parents do not will their most intimate estate.
It passes untraced,
Not in chromosomes only,
But in events too ordinary to remember.
No family group sheet will ever tell us
Which Grandpa Thatcher first bounced a baby to Boston,
Nor will the Post Register record the day
Dad eased Ginger into a gallop in the field
   behind the Rock School
While a little girl in pedalpushers
Clutched his belt in ecstasy and fear.

Fifty years of days.
Standing by the kitchen sink I said to Mother:
"When I grow up I'm going to New York to live."
"New York or Sugar City,"
She answered,
"You still have to eat three meals a day."

She washes a carrot,
Turns it slowly under the tap,
And washes again,
Paring,
Slicing,
("Mary says to cut them on the bias")

As though each chunk were an heirloom.

Another morning,
Sitting on a chair by the kitchen table,
She combing my hair,
I confide a dream.
"You can be anything you want to be,"
She says drily,
"If you are willing to work."

No inventory can account this inheritance.
Dad gave us his smile.
Framed on the end of the buffet
  in the old house in Sugar City,
It warmed us when he was out in the barn
or checking the furnace at the high school
or catching a plane for Boise.
It warms us still.
"We're proud of you," he said.

Mother gave us her content and her discontent.
Her drawer full of recipes,
Unfiled and untried,
Will nourish us when her Empress Beef is forgotten.

WOMAN'S WORK

Real history is always more complex—and interesting—
than stereotypes. Serious study of women's history also
has a way of bridging gaps between generations.

Wanting to know, combined with wanting to do something
positive about knowing, is what allows a worthwhile
performance anywhere—on a committee or project,
at a conference, in a marriage, as a parent.

Laurel Thatcher Ulrich • 1989

A WOMAN'S WORK IS NEVER DONE

WHEN CATHY RICHARDSON WAS asked to give a talk at the
Pursuit of Excellence night in our ward Relief Society, she
wrote a poem instead. A humorous poem. The sisters laughed
and cried.

> *Sweep the house*
> *Make the bread*
> *Never grouse*
> *Smile instead*

> *Make a list*
> *Check the time*
> *Put the wash*
> *Out on the line*

> *Exercise, be tall, be thin*
> *Never let the wrinkles win*

> *Take twenty minutes*
> *for yourself*
> *that's what the experts*
> *say will help*

And so on. Cathy's complaint was therapeutic because she
said what so many women feel. Too many demands, too little
time. Her theme was an old one; her message was fresh and
bleeding.

I have recently finished writing a book on an eighteenth-
century Maine midwife named Martha Ballard. On November
26, 1795, Martha wrote: "I have been doing my house work and
Nursing my cow. Her bag is amazingly sweld." Then she went
on to list the activities of various members of her family, noting
that her hired girls had gone to a neighbor's house where there
was illness. "She returned and Sarah Densmore with her at 11
hour Evening," she continued. "I have been picking wool till

then. A Woman's work is never Done, as the Song says, and happy she whose strength holds out to the end of the race."

Martha Ballard may have been thinking of a seventeenth-century English ballad that begins, "There's never a day, from morn to night, / But I with work am tired quite." Each verse of the old song describes some aspect of a housewife's duties, from spinning wool to feeding a crying baby in the night, ending with the familiar refrain, "A woman's work is never done." The song, of course, was based on an even older proverb, "A man works from sun to sun, but a woman's work is never done."

In the nineteenth century, Mormon women inspired another variant of the old lament.

> Come, girls, come and listen to my noise
> Don't you marry the Mormon boys,
> If you do your fortune it will be
> Johnny Cake n' babies is all you'll see.
>
> Build a little house and put it on a hill,
> Make you work against your will,
> Buy a little cow and milk it in a gourd,
> Put it in a corner and cover it with a board.

In this not-so-charitable account, the misguided woman who married a "Mormon boy" had only herself to blame.

My favorite version of the overburdened housewife's complaint is a poem attributed to Ruth Belknap, the wife of a Dover, New Hampshire minister. She was apparently tired of having her fancy Boston friends talk about the joys of country living. Her poem, written in 1782, was entitled, "The Pleasures of a Country Life . . . written when I had a true taste of them by having no maid."

> Up in the morning I must rise
> Before I've time to rub my eyes.
> With half-pin'd gown, unbuckled shoe,
> I haste to milk my lowing cow.
> But, Oh! it makes my heart to ake,
> I have no bread till I can bake.

The poem goes on to describe the horrors of the dye pot, the terrors of mosquitoes, and the indignities of butchering day ("See me look like ten thousand sluts, My kitchen spread with grease & guts."), ending with a jaunty couplet:

> Come, see the sweets of country life,
> Display'd in Parson B[elknap's] wife.

I don't know if it is any comfort to Cathy Richardson to know that two hundred years ago a woman who lived just across the river from where she lives now felt just as harried as she does.

Why is it that, despite changes in household technology, women still feel overburdened? The life of my Maine midwife shows that the so-called "double burden" is not new at all. Women in pre-industrial America juggled as many demands as women do today, working very hard in and outside their homes as spinners, weavers, dairy-women, chair caners, midwives, nurses, horticulturists, and teachers as well as housekeepers and mothers. If our lives are so much easier, why do we still feel cumbered?

I'm not sure of the answer to that question. Maybe it has to do with a certain mind-set common to middle-class women in many centuries, a female version of the "Protestant work ethic." We feel besieged and miserable because of a compulsive need to fill every minute with productive effort; yet, we are unable, because of the very nature of our work and the gender relations that structure it, to see a product. Think of that ubiquitous commodity, dinner. Now you see it; now you don't.

My own study of Martha Ballard's diary suggests another reason. By its very nature, women's work has been service-oriented, directed toward nurturing and sustaining others. For that reason alone, it is "never done." I am not just talking about jobs like sewing shirts or providing meals, but about a more subtle psychological task—maintaining a continual awareness of and concern for others. The difference is obvious in men's and women's diaries from the eighteenth and early nineteenth centuries. Farmers' diaries from New England tend to be very task-oriented. "Hayed the south field." The women's diaries I have studied are people-oriented. Some part of Martha Ballard's work, for example, was simply noting the welfare and whereabouts of others—her husband, sons, daughters, household helpers, and neighbors. As a consequence, her work spilled over into every cranny of her farm and town.

I am wary of theories that assume rigid differences between men and women, especially those that make little allowance for changes through time. Yet, there really is a remarkable unity in the laments of harried housewives across the centuries. I'm not sure the problem has a whole lot to do with housework. Popular periodicals have begun to carry similar stories about overworked career women. Unfortunately, the message in the magazines seems to be: "You're doing too much. Combining family and job is too great a burden. Quit before you get that mysterious, debilitating disease whispered about in our precincts, 'the young career woman's syndrome.' It strikes working women who are also mothers."

That argument suggests that what you do is the problem. Yet, even the briefest look at the lives of full-time mothers like Cathy Richardson would dispel that notion. The problem is far more complex. I suspect that it has to do with the deepest elements of our socialization as women. Everything in our upbringing and experience teaches us to be responsible and caring, dutiful and kind, but no one teaches us how to set boundaries to our duties—that is, to work from sun to sun.

After all, doesn't the Bible say, "Her candle goeth not out by night." Another eighteenth-century woman, Esther Burr, worried about that passage. She finally decided that it had been misconstrued. A well-made candle wouldn't die on its own, she argued, but a righteous woman knew when to snuff it. Her insight is still useful.

MILK AND HONEY MOTHERHOOD

OVER A DECADE AGO OUR writing committee on the General
Board of the MIA (a not-bad name, Mutual Improvement
Association!) rewrote the manuals for all six age groups—two
years each of Beehive, Mia Maid, and Laurel lessons. I remember writing one for Mia Maids based on Erich Fromm's concept
of mother love in *The Art of Loving*. When it came to a mother
teaching a daughter about sex, he said, lucky was the daughter
whose mother had a sense of self. In that case, he claimed, it
wouldn't matter if the mother said babies came from the
moon—everything would be all right.

The mother with a sense of self was a milk-and-honey
mother. Milk is food at the table, clothes for the back, shelter
for sleep and growth, but honey is the marveling at spring, a
bird, a snowflake, being ready to laugh as well as cry, being a
respondent to the miracles of being alive.

I loved writing that concept into a lesson on what to look
forward to in motherhood. Thinking about it now, I love having had that as subliminal masterminding for whatever happened in subsequent years with my own five daughters and me.
Goodness knows how busy those years were. We had only two
telephone lines with four teenagers, a realtor/bishop husband,
and me in graduate school, on the General Board, teaching
part-time in the university English Department, and coaching
the University of Utah women's tennis team. The phones were
simply symbolic of what in the world was buzzing in and out
of our home in those hectic but wildly satisfying years.
Beneath, around, and above it all, I loved mothering, felt
authentic in it, longed mostly for more time to indulge it.

But time was not, happily, the only index of our finding
each other when we needed to. And by then it probably had a
lot more to do with honey than with milk. Being what we were
for each other was a matter of letting the honey flow—laughing
with each other over recitals, crying over break-ups, talking

ideas while stirring gravy, rehashing a night out at 2 A.M., planning on a ski lift or on the boat, complaining to each other during a work party, or cleaning up after a trip. Never out of touch—literally—much of our honey flowed between hugs and good night kisses and xoxoxo's on letters as our chicks flew the nest.

When my own mother died, the *Ensign* asked me to write about mother/daughter relationships. What a joke. Whoever could come up with anything even close to definitive about that elusive and always challenging connection? But I tried— two days after my mother died, because I could use her as my beacon. The piece concluded with, "May my five girls grow up as I did, with love, Mother."

That was twelve years ago. They have grown up, married, had babies of their own. But the mothering, the pouring out of milk and mixing in of honey never changes. Maybe it's the ongoingness of it that continues to be so compelling. This winter the storms that my mother prayed away as she tapped the pioneer barometer on the front wall have been raging—for one a struggle with novitiate teaching of English in an 80 percent minority intermediate school; for another, three months in bed with a precarious pregnancy; for another, the healing of a child in a disfiguring accident; for another, the displacement of new homes and new jobs; and for another—hardest of all—the ending of a marriage while love still lasts.

One week, fifteen of the eighteen family members were sick; my husband was rushed to the emergency room, dehydrated and with hepatitis suspected. The rest of the winter continued the same theme: swinging back and forth between sickbeds, from Salt Lake to Portland; trying to teach our Institute class with Carlisle Hunsaker on Thursday nights, "Mormon Doctrine and Philosophy for Women"; and for sanity, trying to sandwich in a national senior tennis tournament on my home courts.

Then the well ran dry. The flu took over, and I was the one in the hospital. My daughters covered for me. They cancelled my ridiculous commitments, smoothed my pillow, and held my hand. In my dim and not happy days of submission, too drained to care about much, I realized what honey those girls had been for me forever—that laughing, crazy, reaching, finding, holding, yes, sometimes crying connection to the Spring that must surely lie under all that dirty gray snow on the ground since November. As women they are my "source" even as they were when they were little girls. And now I have sons-in-law as well "to liven like a barrage of salt / these years trembling with passing." To say nothing of another generation buzzing with sweetness and challenge.

As I return to a world I have scarcely looked at in three weeks of post-viral exhaustion and the most I have ever known of depression, I come to this page thinking of mothers and daughters, and I know where the bounty lies. Not in easy flow, which has sometimes been hilariously fun, but in the wrenching and floundering. The covering for each other, the knowing that whenever and whatever, the other will be there—the sisters, the daughters, the finally and forever friends who once occupied my womb, always my life, and someday will occupy whatever waits where Mother is.

In all of it, I recognize more than I ever have the ongoing power of love between generations, between a Father and Mother in Heaven and me—faltering or flourishing—least able or most deserving of milk and honey anything.

POOR MOTHER

WE HAVE A NEW BABY in our family. Soon after Amy was born, our oldest son introduced himself to the woman who was building a house behind ours.

"And how many children are there in your family?" she asked politely.

"Five," he answered. "I'm fifteen. My brother and sister are in junior high. Thatcher is in first grade, and my baby sister is just three weeks old."

"Your poor mother!" the woman gasped. "She's got them spread all over the place."

She herself has birds—twenty-eight of them inhabit a glass aviary built into the living room of her hexagonal house. When she and her husband want to go away for a weekend, she hires my daughter (at $2.50 a day) to scoop a ration of worms from the box in the refrigerator each morning before school and return again at bedtime to see that none of her feathered specimens is hanging upside down from a perch. She pays 50 cents extra for watering the philodendron.

"Aren't you noble," she said sardonically on our first meeting, after asking again: "How many children do you have?" We climbed the circular stair to her book-lined loft where she showed me her typewriter, and her seven published volumes. "We have one bedroom in this house," she said, pointing to the extra mattress which can be pulled out from under the eaves if needed. Perhaps her next book will be about birds. There are six about horses, one about ships, and two children's stories in manuscript on her publisher's desk.

My children like our new neighbor, especially since she invited them to sled on her long unshoveled driveway. "Anytime after eleven."

Perhaps on closer acquaintance I will like her too. But for the moment she remains the Bird Lady and I the Woman with the Green Tomato Mincemeat and the Kids. I didn't want to disillusion her by telling her I too had a study and a typewriter. She had stereotyped me before we met—and I her. Would it surprise her to know that some mornings I manage to sit for three hours at a time reading Erasmus in my bathrobe in the sun? Perhaps not, but for now I prefer to keep my secret. We all need myths with which to justify and ratify our lives. I went home feeling like the cat who swallowed her canary.

"Your poor mother!" I would once have slithered uncomfortably under that label, suspecting that in both senses it fit. I did feel inadequate to my calling. I did lament my lot. Not now. Yet this is strange, for by anybody's definition Amy was an ill-timed baby. After fifteen years of peanut butter and Legos, my days were about to become open from eight-thirty until three. After a decade of eking out a course here and a course there, I could think about some serious teaching and at last begin research for my dissertation. The house was almost finished, the bedrooms and closets fitted out for four children, and in one corner of the dining room the old iron crib had been converted to an amusing settee. All six of us had bicycles and could ride them, and the worn Hike-a-poose could now be changed to a rucksack for those long-planned treks in the Presidential Range. Certainly in our laddered and lofted castle in the woods there was no room for an infant.

Yet along came Amy. The castle has a new Princess and whether it is she or I, I cannot determine. I grow sentimental. I grow saccharine. I can't imagine anything so delightful as a five-month-old baby who sleeps irregularly, eats often, and has already learned to tear the pages of books. I suppress all thought of Terrible Twos and of the possible traumas in coping with one lone teenager at fifty. I revel in her cushioned cheeks and pearled toes.

At different times during the weeks after Amy was born, three friends, all non-Mormons, came by to tell me they were jealous. Their children, corresponding in ages to my older ones, have grown independent. Chauffeuring is their most insistent need. After school their children run to the soccer field with scarcely a glance at the proffered cookie. They take baths, ask to go to dances, and sleep out in igloos carved scientifically in the snow. They criticize their mother's driving and their father's taste in ties. They talk about college and dream of fame. "Are we getting old?" We laughed. "Sometimes I feel as though my only function is to stand at the door and shout: You forgot to make your bed!" We joked about the "empty nest syndrome," compared symptoms, and recognized in each other the same bittersweet pangs. "But you have Amy!" And so I do. My friends will sigh and exclaim over pink noses in the supermarket, but they will go on to practice the harpsichord, begin a master's in nutrition, or take up pharmacy again. And I will raise Amy and be glad.

That bald and toothless infant over there on the floor inching her way to the foot of my study is not Number Five. She is Amy. I think of another friend, a woman of scholarly attainment and demographic conviction. A month ago I met her at a community function. She rushed over to me smiling broadly. "Congratulations!" I must have shown my surprise for throughout my pregnancy she had studiously ignored my condition, so skillfully in fact that I had begun to wonder if the twenty-five extra pounds I was carrying showed. "For getting your article accepted," she finished cheerfully. "Babies don't count." I loved her bluntness and in my own upside-down way I am convinced she is right: "Babies don't count." Amy is my sister and my neighbor and my child and I hope someday she will be my friend, but she is not a rung on my ladder to the celestial kingdom.

Writing this I recognize that articles don't count either. As my friend described her own work, an intricate and incredibly detailed reconstruction of an entire county over three generations, I knew that she knew it too. "The picture is emerging, but it will take us another ten years at least. It doesn't matter. I love it. I live there." Anyone who has faced an academic tenure committee knows the old joke about deans who can count but not read. Occasionally, even on the fringes of the university, with no need to get or hold a job, I am seized with the panic to get my name in print. I am beginning to recognize, however, how those first articles and books can be mere sops to the ego, means to the inner quiet which will allow the slow nurturing of a work of love.

A few weeks ago, my oldest son commented at dinner: "We have four writers in the neighborhood."

"Is that right? Who?" I asked.

"The new neighbor. Mr. Weesner [his first novel was a Book-of-the-Month Club selection]. Mr. Williams [he won the National Book Award last year]. And you." I laughed, though he wasn't teasing, and I knew that he was right.

As I look at Amy, I know that my own self-possession has something to do with the pleasure I feel in her growth. Sometimes when I hear young mothers in our ward lament their inadequacies, talking like the poor mother I used to be, I want to stand up and pontificate: "Get out of the house. Find out what you're good at. Stop feeling sorry for yourself. Learn and grow." But I don't, for I know that I am not a happier and better mother at thirty-seven than I was at twenty-two because I have taken night courses or written essays or read Erasmus, but because at thirty-seven I have begun to understand the fruitful and uneasy and joyful and sometimes terrifying relationship between the woman I am and the woman I would like to be. That kind of learning can neither be hurried nor forced.

A WORD FROM THE WHYS:

LISTENING TO MY TEENAGER

AS IN MOST RELATIONSHIPS that mean anything, it was easy to blow things way out of proportion. My husband and I returned from the family reunion about 8:30 that night, expecting to pick up our sixteen-year-old daughter and go blithely from the hot city to the cool of our cabin to sleep. We had planned it all before we left. She was working, would have gotten home in time, and our evening would be serene and cozy. She had had her one date for the week with John and had assured us that she had "so much to do" that she couldn't come to the reunion, and would be home *alone* all evening until we came to pick her up for our jaunt to the canyon.

So it was with somewhat smug parental astonishment that we found taped to the hood of the kitchen stove a note: "Dear Mom and Dad, John and I decided on the spur to go to an 8:00 movie. Hope you had a good time. I'll be home right after. I love you." It was signed "Megan Katie Thayne," the name she uses only when calling up its ingratiating thoroughness to doting parents who christened her all of that.

A simple enough note, not unlike many taped in that same place by a household of comings and goings over lots of years. But this was the youngest of our five daughters, our last little chick at home, and having her out on whatever town she and some still mysterious young man chose to occupy for an evening seemed suddenly fraught with more than our midlife sense of crisis could handle. Where was she? How could she possibly have presumed to impose this irrational spontaneity on our so-well-planned time? Didn't she know that she needed our permission for this sort of flight? Hadn't she already played tennis, gone swimming, had chats on the lawn, and been on that date this week with John? Didn't she know she was breaking a basic family rule?

And what movie? With all the strains on sense and sensibility around, how did we have any notion of what line they might be in? And what about this John? What did we really know about him—except that he had a good smile and played a great game of water polo, was wry and winning to talk to while he waited for Megan, and, according to her, was "one of the few really good guys at school, even at stomps."

Going to the cabin was now out of the question. The injustice of being suddenly corralled by the impetuosity of a teenage daughter sent us both scurrying into our own outlets for indignation. I began ironing with a vengeance, and Mel turned the TV on to a show he had always hated. An hour passed, then two, almost three. It was getting toward time when any 8:00 show would have long been out, food even at a chew-and-chat rate consumed, and any long-night's journey home charted and completed. I had thought of every infraction of any rule in any book that Megan has ever indulged in any of her sixteen years on earth. Mel had isolated a dozen penalties, and together we had decided that John was not only two years older, but worthless, maybe even dangerous, and Megan was worse. There would be no taking the car, no going out even with her friends, and meals were definitely in jeopardy.

But luckily at twenty-seven minutes to twelve, when I went to mail a letter, I had a chance to sit alone in a dark car in the driveway and ponder a few things. One was something my father had told me and illustrated time and again: Never start talking until you've listened for at least as long as you plan to talk. Another came just as urgently to pound in my head: Wonder a little about *why* as well as *what* in any situation.

And then up popped the prize, an outgrowth of both of the above: Everything good that is ever accomplished has come about because of someone's *constructive* curiosity.

I sat in the car and let myself drift, slowly, I admit, into constructive curiosity. And as I did, I began to wonder all right. About Megan. About how she felt. About why she'd do something so out of character with what she usually did. About John. About who he really was. About what they were for each other—and about what an 8:00 show on the spur might have meant to two kids on a Saturday night.

Out of my wondering came some remembering. I went in and began telling Mel about when I was sixteen. I remembered being on the sandy shore of Bear Lake dancing to a blaring jukebox with my boyfriend—a boy my mother never exactly liked. Mel remembered his two-hour phone conversations with a girl discussing "The Hit Parade," hiding in a broom closet from a father who would have pushed buttons on any conversation over three minutes. "And look how terrific we turned out!" we laughingly agreed.

In a quarter hour of wondering, of chuckling and remembering, we discovered more about each other's sixteen-year-old behavior than we had known in twenty-eight years of living together. And, luckily, our sense of proportion and of humor came racing to rescue us.

At 12:02 the lights of the front window told us John's Bronco was in the driveway and Mel, convenient coward that he is, said, "Why don't you have a girl-to-girl chat with her and let me know what in the world she's thinking." That seemed a good plan actually—one-on-one, not two-on-one.

And we did, Megan and I. We had a fine chat. One of the best ever. She came in smiling—if a bit docile—wondering herself what our reaction to her almost-forgotten note would be. Thank goodness my anger had been quelled by curiosity, my curiosity piqued by a genuine concern for making things better, not worse.

Just as constructive curiosity had pulled me out of myself, my interest touched off interest in her—for *me*. And although we covered some pretty uncomfortable topics, it was with a sense of discovery, of searching out a path that both of us could occupy and travel with our feelings for ourselves and for each other in positive order.

First, I listened for at least as long as I thought I might like to talk—quite a while. I found out *why*, not just *what*. Megan had gotten off work early, a rare happiness. And with her hair wet from a marvelous shower on a hot late afternoon, she had heard from John. There was a good show on, and he too, by the coincidence native only to high school confederates, had gotten off work early. "I knew you'd understand," she said, "the way things just work out sometimes, and I figured I'd just do what I'd do if you were here. Isn't that what you always say to do?" She had me—by my own inclinings.

I was intrigued. By the time we had gone through the getting there and the show they had arrived too late to get in and so had had to go to another (one which I definitely wanted to hear *all* about) we were both primed for a real talk—one about the whys of more than just going to the show: Why John? Why a thousand feelings new to young pulses and dispositions? Why a disregard for sixteen years of living with our household's particular particulars? Why a one-night imposition of one upon the other? And for her—*why* our worry? *Why* rules anyhow? *What* for the future?

By the time it was my turn to "talk," we had worked our way through so much that needed to be said that I had nothing to "say"—only hugs to give and private arrivals to cherish. And assurance to nudge into a sleepy husband that what had been fostered had been restoration rather than rebellion—for both of us.

Going to sleep I wondered a little, of course, if I had been "strict" enough. What rule-ridden parent wouldn't? And then I thought of Mark's interpolation on the Savior's golden rule: "And to love [her] with all the heart, and with all the understanding" (Mark 12:33). The understanding that can come only through constructive curiosity. Like loving, it is the great freer.

Today I'll be free to wonder about new things—about how to hit a better forehand or coax some life into a geranium that got too dry, or prepare more ably for a Sunday School lesson, or an afternoon with a grandchild. And I rather think that constructive curiosity can enliven any relationship I want to build—with a friend, in a classroom, with that aunt who is doing battle with a too crowded past and an uninhabited present.

Wanting to know, combined with wanting to do something positive about knowing, is what allows a worthwhile performance anywhere—on a committee or project, at a conference, in a marriage, as a parent. It is what persuades enlightened reading of a scripture or a balance sheet. It is what must be behind every productive conversion, diet, sale, or probe into the unknown. It is the way to build any kingdom, on earth or in heaven. Constructive curiosity can impel and illuminate every getting up, getting done, falling in love, or making amends. It is the secret in any meaningful meeting or prayer.

Letting constructive curiosity work last night with Megan was not miring us in the soft sand of permissiveness, but supplying us a footing in the firm clay of understanding. She came to know the reasons behind our concern and our rules and, I think, to respect them both. And I hope maybe another Saturday night . . . Well, who really knows? But I do know I've been graced by an insight I'd like to cling to, one I wish could rub off on those children of ours just as my father's notions glazed me last night.

Come to think of it, I do believe Megan actually wanted to know when she asked this morning after Sunday School, "By the way, Dad, how did your lesson go?" At least she seemed to be listening all the time she was dialing her best friend's number.

GOOD-BYE, VIRGINIA SLIMS

LAST SEMESTER I ASKED the students in an introductory women's history course to write a short paper comparing their own lives with their mothers' lives at the same age. Before we launched into a discussion of the early twentieth-century transition from the "Gibson Girl" to the "Flapper," I wanted them to be aware of the complexities in tracing historical change across generations. For most of the class, the assignment worked well. One young woman, however, surprised me by handing in an unfocused paper, far beneath the quality of her usual work.

"This doesn't sound like you," I wrote on the bottom of her essay. "Did you have trouble with the assignment?"

A few days later she came in to ask if she could rewrite her paper. "I think I am feeling more objective about it now," she said, "but last week I was too upset about my conversation with my mother to really think about what I was saying." I felt a flash of guilt at having imposed that kind of burden on a student, and I began to wonder about the ethical limitations of the sort of assignment I had given. Fortunately, for this student (I'll call her Lisa), the ultimate outcome was positive. After our talk, she rewrote her paper, and she indicated that she felt much better able to handle the conflict in her own life.

Lisa's problem was pretty straightforward. She had done things her mother had never had the opportunity to do. The more competent and independent she became, the more diminished and inconsequential her mother felt. Lisa's mother had dropped out of school to marry, had given birth to five or six children, and though some of the children were still at home, was now working full-time at a low-paying job to help sustain her husband's business. Lisa loved and respected her mother, yet when she told her she wanted to ask her some questions about her early life, her mother simply snapped, "Why? So you can see how much better off you are than me?"

Americans have long assumed that each generation will be

taller, better educated, and more successful than the last. For women's history, the myth of progress has been popularized in the Virginia Slims ads. These ads exaggerate women's disabilities in the past and the extent of their freedom today. In the bad old days, they say, women were hemmed in by domineering husbands, tight corsets, and repressive social conventions. Now we are free to wear hot pants, smoke cigarettes, and climb to the top of the corporate ladder. Even those of my students who question the triumphant hedonism of Virginia Slims accept the underlying philosophy of the ads. The past, they believe, can be measured in terms of the present. They may prefer other criteria—admissions to law school, for example—but they believe in progress nonetheless.

The casualties of such a philosophy are not only women like Lisa's mother but sometimes their daughters as well. Most of us know young women who feel overwhelmed rather than liberated by the supposed freedoms they enjoy. The classic description of this situation is in *Twenty Years at Hull House* where Jane Addams describes a mother and daughter she met at a French pension in the 1880s. The mother was happy in the belief that she had given her daughter opportunities she had never had herself, yet the daughter "looked back upon her mother's girlhood with positive envy because it was so full of happy industry and extenuating obstacles." Given unlimited opportunity to develop her musical talent, the girl began to doubt its existence. She was "simply smothered and sickened with advantages."

The idea that the present should be measured by the past is just as demoralizing as its opposite. The flip side of "We've come a long way, baby" is the cinnamon-laden domesticity Pepperidge Farm remembers. According to this version of history, mothers lived in the kitchen and loved it. There is no unrealized ambition in this story, no poverty or smallpox, just good-tasting bread and cookies hot from the oven. Mormon women may prefer this brick-oven-baked sentiment to cigarettes, but between two slick versions of women's past there is really little to choose. The sepia tones of Pepperidge Farm are every bit as fake as those of Virginia Slims.

The irony is that both ads employ visual imagery from the early twentieth century, an age of remarkable transformation in women's lives. In the period between 1890 and 1920, ordinary women baked cakes and stitched quilts to support social reform while college-educated women helped to create the new professions of social work and public health. Famous women like Jane Addams and ordinary women like my grandmother Siddoway built kindergartens, attacked drunkenness, created parks and playgrounds, fought lynching, founded labor unions, and set up milk stations for the poor. They earned the right to vote not only through political activism but by celebrating women's traditional strengths. What the United States needed, they argued, was "urban housekeeping." If women knew how to sweep out dirt, why not crime?

So much for the downtrodden—or contentedly domestic—women of 1910. My mother has a picture of Grandma Siddoway in her Gibson Girl waist and divided skirt ready to mount her horse, Old Jack. Grandma carries the cigar box in which she kept the receipts of the Teton City School Board of which she was the clerk. Although she died before I was born, Grandma Siddoway was a wonderful cook as well as an efficient treasurer of the Fremont County Republican party. I have her white linen tablecloths, her recipe for piccalilli, and a heritage of public service.

Real history is always more complex—and interesting—than stereotypes. Serious study of women's history also has a way of bridging gaps between generations. In oral history workshops, in community projects, in classrooms, and in living rooms, I have seen women reach across the years to each other with surprising sensitivity and skill. If women's history is seen as an effort to comprehend difference, to discover possibilities and perplexities unlike our own, rather than as a long march upward (or downward) into the present, we become free to compare without intimidating. I have noticed that as my students abandon the Virginia Slims mentality with which many of them enter a course, they begin to appreciate the complexity of women's lives in every historical period, and often they find models of courage and resourcefulness they never would have considered before. Most lives have both extenuating obstacles and undiscovered opportunities. Seeing these in the lives of other women often helps us to recognize them in our own.

RIP OFF

Call me mother! Call me daughter!
Call me wife! Call me friend!
Rip off a splinter. Here.
Post it to some slick daily pole
to cling to. But watch
how it ribbons with red despair
your holiness. A splinter
is unnative as misery. Coarse sawdust
from nowhere. Never really offered like leaves
in fall knowing spring.
Torn away.

And what it is ripped off of
is shriveled, reduced to definition
like a peeled apple by its standing,
as the pulling at the scrawny frays
twirls me shredded
in the tactless wind of waning.

The proffered shards, puny as intention,
whip me this way and that
untouchable
between the devouring breaths
of time and circumstance
and wanting to be
enough.

But the stripping
has laid not one solid branch
to any hand.
Only scrupulous splinters.

And splinters, even gathered in the perpetual force
of love,
are never allowed
the heroism of roots
or the biding bend of the mountain wind
or the vineyard fingers of rising spring.

A HISTORY LESSON

MY STUDENTS HAVE A hard time understanding why women's suffrage seemed so threatening in the years before 1920. Then I showed them my collection of antisuffrage cartoons from the magazine *Life*. Seeing the suffragists stereotyped as man-haters, as generals in the war between the sexes, they more easily grasp the power of the antisuffrage rhetoric. Who wouldn't prefer a "true woman" (often a lovely Charles Dana Gibson girl) to a beefy old-maid feminist?

The antisuffragists argued that God had decreed an eternal specialization of function for men and for women. Giving women the vote threatened "the old and natural order" established "when Adam was put in the Garden of Eden to dress it and keep it, and Eve was given to him as a helpmeet." Women were not inferior to men; they were simply different. Furthermore, their responsibilities in the home were so demanding, so central, that to add the burden of voting could only result in neglect of the family. Beyond that, most women did not *want* the vote. Only misguided women, women who had lost the true sense of their own worth, would demand the privileges of men.

The logic was compelling. Because men voted and women didn't, women who wanted to vote wanted to be men. And because men had the power to give or withhold suffrage, women who asked for the vote attacked men. Because men and women were seen as sovereigns over separate territories, any crossing of borders constituted an invasion—or a capitulation. By definition, a gain for women meant a loss for men.

If the arguments seem familiar—and surprisingly current—so do the rebuttals. The prosuffragists countered that certain fundamental rights and responsibilities belonged to the human species rather than to men or women in particular. Because female and male were both created in the image of God, exaggerating the differences between them led to the atrophy of virtues that really belonged to both. Women needed to be strong as well as loving; men needed to care as well as to act. Nor was true companionship possible when one partner was unnaturally dependent upon the other. As suffragist Anna Howard Shaw put it, "They who observe more closely the sturdy oak about which the ivy clings, find it dead at the top."

In response to the religious argument, the suffragists said that God's statement that Adam should rule over Eve was a prediction, not a command. Men *had* dominated women, to the detriment of both, but in an enlightened society that kind of behavior had no place. No one argued that the curse of Adam prevented men from inventing machinery to lighten their labor. Preventing women from enlarging their powers was equally absurd. Christ had come to redeem all mankind— women as well as men. Male dominance belonged to a fallen world in which men earned their bread with a bow and arrow or a wooden plow.[1]

It is pleasant to remember that at the time of the *Life* cartoons, the question of woman suffrage had long been settled in Utah. Mormon women had first voted in 1870, had lost the right in 1884 under the Edmunds-Tucker Act, and had won it again in 1896 at statehood. But as Jean Bickmore White has shown, the question of woman's place was bitterly debated in Utah's constitutional convention of 1896.[2] By the 1890s, some prominent Mormon leaders, including B.H. Roberts, the Seventy and historian, had accepted the logic of the antisuffrage movement. Roberts insisted that votes for women would undermine the fundamental differences between the sexes: "Let me say that the influence of woman as it operates upon me never came from the rostrum, it never came from the pulpit, with woman in it, it never came from the lecturer's platform, with woman speaking; it comes from the fireside, it comes from the blessed association with mothers, of sisters, of wives, of daughters, not as democrats or republicans."[3]

Roberts opposed woman suffrage on principle. Others worried that including it in the state constitution would once again delay Utah's bid for statehood. Fortunately there were Mormon leaders at the constitutional convention who knew how to counter such concerns. Orson F. Whitney invoked the millennialist optimism of early Mormonism in support of the women's cause. "This great social upheaval, this woman's movement that is making itself heard and felt, means something more than that certain women are ambitious to vote and hold office," he said. "I regard it as one of the great levers by which the Almighty is lifting up this fallen world, lifting it nearer to the throne of its Creator."[4]

Franklin D. Richards said that if winning statehood meant the "disenfranchisement of one half the people," then he would be content to share "territorial vassalage" with Utah's women until the time came when "all can stand side by side on the broad platform of human equality, of equal rights, and of equal capacity."[5] Songs from the *Utah Woman Suffrage Songbook* echo that theme. In the great cause of equality men and women must stand side by side. "Come brothers, sisters, join the strain and swell it sweet and strong," went the chorus of one campaign song inviting men as well as women "to wave the flag of equal rights in Utah."

They did. Women passed petitions; men pushed the clause through the convention; and Utah came into the union in 1896 with woman suffrage in the constitution. There were only three other states in which women already had the vote (Wyoming, Idaho, and Colorado). There wouldn't be another until 1910. As late as 1914 (when the *Life* cartoons appeared), not a single state east of the Mississippi allowed women to vote in general elections.

For many years Utah and the other western states who allowed women to vote were considered "freak states." Ardent suffragists considered them a vanguard. For Mormons the notion of being "in the van" of human progress was familiar. Louisa Greene Richards, the founding editor of the *Woman's Exponent*, wrote a song for the Utah suffrage songbook that urged women to "Seize the scepter, hold the van, Equal with thy brother, man." Meekness was inappropriate for daughters of God called to usher in a new world of peace and love.

The undisguised self-assertion of her song continues to astonish and chasten those of us who wonder whether we are

134

part of a freak minority or a saving remnant. Since Claudia Bushman first introduced us to it, "Woman Arise" has become a favorite at annual retreats held in Hillsboro, New Hampshire, for staff and readers of *Exponent II*.

Woman, Arise
(Sung to the tune of "Hope of Israel")

Freedom's daughter, rouse from slumber,
See the curtains are withdrawn
Which so long thy mind hath shrouded
Lo! thy day begins to dawn.

Chorus

Woman, 'rise, thy penance o'er,
Sit thou in the dust no more;
Seize the scepter, hold the van,
Equal with thy brother, man.

Truth and virtue be thy motto,
Temp'rance, liberty and peace.
Light shall shine and darkness vanish.
Love shall reign, oppression cease.

Chorus

First to fall 'mid Eden's bowers,
Through long suff'ring worthy proved,
With the foremost claim thy pardon,
When earth's curse shall be removed.

Chorus

At Hillsboro Camp we may be literally sitting in the dust, or at least in the pine needles under a tree, but we have gotten into the habit of scrambling to our feet at the beginning of the chorus in respect for our nineteenth-century sisters—and brothers. It is enlivening to remember that historic moment, almost a century ago, when the women and men of Zion together lifted the banner of equality.

Note

[1]The above discussion is based on Aileen S. Kraditor, *The Ideas of the Woman Suffrage Movement*, (New York: 1981).

[2]Jean Bickmore White, "Women's Place Is in the Constitution: The Struggle for Equal Rights in Utah in 1895," *Utah Historical Quarterly*, 42 (Fall 1974): p. 344-369.

[3]Quoted in White, p. 358.

[4]White, p. 359.

[5]White, p. 369.

STORMS

Utah Cabin
Thursday, 8:30 A.M.

Yesterday afternoon as I shopped for birthday hiking boots with my twelve-year-old grandson, Coulson, a young pretty blonde woman came screaming into Mervyn's suburban main floor. She was dirt-smeared and bleeding from her jaw and legs, white socks minus shoes, white long shorts and T-shirt blotched and torn. A store employee guided her by the arm to the elevator, not two feet from where we gaped in disbelief.

"What . . . ?" I started to ask.

"She's been attacked," was all the woman at her elbow said.

In the parking lot? In broad daylight? Could this be real? The wild fear in her eyes and her trembling will echo across our memories as no TV or movie depiction ever could.

Near us a girl about eight with her mother and little sister sobbed uncontrollably. As I tried to reassure her, squeeze her shoulder and say how many kind and good people were all around to help, her mother said that her daughter had been attacked once too and was way past frightened in seeing it again.

Last night Coulson was lying under the big quilt on the bed in the living room of the cabin. On my way upstairs to read stories to his three little brothers, I sat by him and asked how he was doing.

"I remember the lady, Gramma."

"It was pretty awful wasn't it?" I said, rubbing his arm and cheek.

"Yeah. Was she for sure going to be okay?"

We had seen the paramedics arriving as we left the store. "I hope so," I said. "And that little girl too. It's pretty scary to see violence up close."

"Yeah. Makes you want to never see it again. Who'd do a thing like that anyhow?"

Who knows. But I'd give anything to be able to keep it from happening again—to anybody. Any ideas, Laurel?

Durham, New Hampshire
Friday, 9 A.M.

When your Fax arrived I was reading the *Boston Globe*. There was a story in the Metro section about a man who agreed to head a Boston commission on teen violence after his own son— an honor student and Eagle Scout—was shot down on his way home from school. Until his son's death, the new commission- er had thought teenage crime was somebody else's problem, that concentrating on his own children was the best way to deal with it. When the violence struck his son, he realized that violence was everybody's problem.

I thought about that when I read your story about the attack in Mervyn's. How depressing! You and Coulson start on a happy errand and end up face-to-face with ugliness. It makes me want to hunker down under a big quilt, like Coulson did, and never come out. But you've written about that before, how we have to keep on pouring out milk and honey while the storms rage inside or outside our cabins. One thing is certain. Whether or not we take on the world's problems, they have a way of finding us.

Utah Cabin
Saturday, 1 P.M.

Yes the storms do come. And don't we need our resources! Here at the cabin I have the old stereo with records (remember them?) playing "Try to Remember." And I'm remembering. Though I feel exactly as I did at fifteen or forty, I find others help me in new ways as I grow into the next stage. You and I talk a lot about our families and our work, but what would we do or be without our friends? Those everywhere on our common branch.

I just opened another package from my once Catholic friend Barbara Duree of Chicago—books, four of them, advance uncorrected galleys that she reviews for *American Library Booklist*. Every few weeks a new batch comes, under- lined, annotated, always exactly right for me in sickness and in

138

health. She's a furnisher. Like family.

Yet when I visited my ninety-seven-year-old friend dying of pneumonia, our friendship counted for very little with the hospital personnel. In our almost daily visits Margaret still asked me for the hug we'd always had, and we laughed at her needing so often the "Damitol" pills I'd found for her last birthday. Loved, but long since a widow, married for the first time at sixty-five, she had no children of her own, was the last leaf on her family tree. At the nurse's station when I asked if she could have something for pain, the question was, "Are you family?" I was not the daughter she never had. Nor a professional. "No," I heard myself saying, "I'm only a friend." Not eligible to request relief. What nonsense! Think of the succor we receive from friends.

Barbara in Chicago has no children, not even a family in the LDS sense of the word. She takes in animals in trouble, is a St. Francis of Assisi to birds and cats and a giant German shepherd. And to causes and charities. Her "multiplying and replenishing" has to do more with spirit than numbers. And her friends, like lucky me, are fed ideas and affection and good humor as well as a sense of worth by her generosity. Out of one of the latest books she sent me, *Fermi Buffalo*, poems by eighty-three-year-old poet Louise McNeill, a stanza from "On Reflection without Color":

> *In His image we were made.*
> *In his likeness formed divine.*
> *I am white, but you are yellow;*
> *You are gold, but I am sallow;*
> *Search the pale prismatic line—*
> *Is God's color yours or mine?*

Differences, Laurel. And gifts from everywhere, as I know you know. In age, in the geography of our lives, I value more the differences as I grow into some of the realities of aging.

Durham, New Hampshire
Monday, 8:30 A.M.

Funny that you should write just now about the burdens of

aging and the need for friends. This morning, while I sit at my computer trying to write my way into the day, my mother is marooned in a hospital bed, her dementia worsening while her broken hip mends. Every day she asks me where she is and how she got there.

Saturday when I arrived, she was lying quietly in bed.

"Hi, Mom," I said.

Her eyes brightened, then closed. "Please help me," she said in the small, whining voice that is so much a part of her now.

"How can I help you?" I asked, speaking softly, directly into her ear as the nurses at the Alzheimer's unit had taught me.

"Don't let things fall on me," she said.

For two weeks I've been trying to hold up her sky. Forgetting to eat, unable to sleep, I have been negotiating with nurses, social workers, and hard-to-find doctors, trying to keep Mother happy in the hospital while scrambling to find a rehabilitation facility that can deal with her confusion and tantrums as well as her broken bone. Yesterday I was a crumpled wreck, not sure I could get through breakfast, let alone a typical Sunday.

As we drove to church, Mindy, visiting for the weekend, said, "Mom, you can't take on all of Grandma's pain without destroying yourself." I came home, took three Advil, and pulled the covers over my head.

Last night my friend Nancy Bussey and her husband, Laury, visited Mother in the hospital. Nancy is a nurse, a wonderfully wise and caring nurse who put her arms around me after Relief Society and told me it was time to relax my vigil. She called later to tell me how the visit went.

Mother was lying quietly in bed when they arrived. They thought she was sleeping, but as they approached, she opened her eyes and said, "Who is it?"

They introduced themselves and began to chat. Laury, skimming through a scrapbook I had made, found a program from the Sugar City Ladies Chorus, circa 1950. He got mother talking about Sugar City and music.

"Shall we sing together," Laury asked. When Nancy suggested "O My Father," a window opened in my mother's mind and she recited the first verse from memory:

O my Father, thou that dwellest
In the high and glorious place,
When shall I regain thy presence
And again behold thy face?

Nancy said it was hard to get through the song because she and Laury were both weeping. Afterwards, they fed Mother a Ritz cracker with peanut butter and told her they would come again.

Utah Cabin
Tuesday, 10 A.M.

I ache for your mother and for you. What's harder than seeing someone we love suffer? Let alone disappear into that dimness that shuts out even a daughter and lets in only a distant past.

I have been thinking today about the gift of life, how sometimes overburdened it can become, regardless of our regard for it. And how little we sometimes know of what really creates or perpetuates those burdens for even our closest. And how unqualified I am to judge anyone else's wrestling with that burdening. Two of my attempts to understand are in the next section: in a funeral talk for a friend who burdened herself beyond endurance; the other about the very private struggles of women with what persuades their giving life or not. I think of Micah 6:8, one of my favorites, "What doth the Lord require of thee, but to do justly, and to love mercy, and to walk humbly with thy God?"

Durham, New Hampshire
Wednesday, 9:15 A.M.

Yes, walk humbly, and through Christ's love, extend mercy even to ourselves.

ON THE SIDE OF LIFE

It was a kind of Pentecost that for a moment dissolved the boundaries between heaven and earth and between present and past. . . . I would gladly sift through a great trough of meal for even a little bit of that leaven.

How to make peace with so much that conspires to trap us all—doubt, inability, bewilderment at having too much or too little, guilt over not being enough?

ON THE SIDE OF LIFE

OUR FOURTH DAUGHTER called two days ago after her visit to her obstetrician. "The baby's dropped, Mom, everything's perfect—in position, all set. And he says it weighs about seven pounds! Be ready to come!"

What could be more exciting? At ages twenty-six and twenty-eight, the new mother and father would welcome that first baby like little else they had ever welcomed.

Three months ago our third daughter had her third child, a boy, perfect. Another person ready to flourish in a home where he would be loved and nurtured. And we would be grandparents relishing this stage of baby-loving in a far from empty nest.

At almost the same hour a friend's daughter had a baby girl with spina bifida—a spinal column unclosed. It was a first child for the daughter, a first grandchild for my friend. Three weeks and three operations later, my friend wept into the phone, "How can we stand to see that little baby suffer any more? The little thing cried so much she hardly had a voice when she came out of that operating room with tubes everywhere. And no matter what they do, the doctor tells us she'll never be functional—in fact, she'll be a vegetable. And so much pain."

Still another week later, "Her own doctor, who's a stake president, says for my daughter to go ahead and get pregnant again, as soon as they can, and hope for a well baby. But in the second month they can tell if it's spina bifida and can abort. He said that no one could think it anything but merciful."

The mysteries. The contradictions. The claims and counterclaims. The personal experience together with the marches, the declarations, the court decisions. The media reporting attacks on Planned Parenthood clinics, and alarming injunctions by religious leaders against abortion on demand, as "heinous birth control, murder." *The Silent Scream*, a film considered medical certainty by some, and quackery—distorted and propagandistic—by others. The question of when life begins is a new variety of

THE MOTHER [1]
by Gwendolyn Brooks

Abortions will not let you forget.
You remember the children you got that you did not get.
The damp small pulps with a little or with no hair,
The singers and workers that never handled the air.
You will never neglect or beat
Them, or silence or buy with a sweet.
You will never wind up the sucking-thumb
Or scuttle off ghosts that come.
You will never leave them, controlling your luscious sigh,
Return for a snack of them,with gobbling mother-eye.

I have heard in the voices of the wind the voices of my dim killed children.
I have contracted. I have eased
My dim dears at the breasts they could never suck.
I have said, Sweets, if I sinned, if I seized
Your luck
And your lives from your unfinished reach,
If I stole your births and your names,
Your straight baby tears and your games,
Your stilted or lovely loves, your tumults, your marriages, aches, and your deaths,
If I poisoned the beginnings of your breaths,
Believe that even in my deliberateness I was not deliberate.
Though why should I whine,
Whine that the crime was other than mine?—
Since anyhow you are dead.
Or rather, or instead,
You were never made.
But that too, I am afraid,
Is faulty: oh, what shall I say, how is the truth to be said?
You were born, you had body, you died.
It is just that you never giggled or planned or cried.

Believe me, I loved you all.
Believe me, I knew you, though faintly, and I loved, I loved you
All.

hype that has divided the country as few issues have.

All this in the midst of the first widespread concern about the emotional and physical welfare of women betrayed by ill-conceived, ill-fated motherhood. This is a world of active sex and inactive restraint. It is a time for thoughtful weighing of old values against new possibilities.

And what sense can I make of it? What might I do if placed in a situation similar to my friend's daughter's where my unborn child might face a life of tragic deprivation? In confrontation with such sprawling questions as abortion presents, I pray for understanding, kindness, and the wisdom to follow Matthew 7:1–2: "Judge not, that ye be not judged. For with what judgment ye judge, ye shall be judged: and with what measure ye mete, it shall be measured to you again."

Not judging does not mean indifference, indecision, or dis-engagement, but being consciously on the side of life, in each instance struggling to affirm life and at the same time honoring the gift of agency.

I watched my mother die, an experience as awesome as watching our first grandbaby born in a gush of misshapen head, slick body, lumpy grey-white cord, and a *waaah* the shape of the whole birthing room. A boy. Sticklike arms and legs of a boy. Six pounds, thirteen ounces of ears, fingers, belly, bones, and lavender feet long enough to ski on. All moving, part of the exultant squall. Everyone grinning through tears. The wanted baby alive and well. In the moment of his coming alive—*ensoulment*. His animating spark. Awesome. No less awesome my mother's dying. She was seventy-six and bright to the end. As I sat beside her that last day holding her hand, she talked with her eyes closed. For hours her lips moved. When I'd lean close to ask what she was saying, it was apparent it was to someone else, in a sibilant tongue unknown to me. When a tiny nosegay of violets came, I showed them to her. She opened her eyes, smiled, gasped, and was gone. Her life, ardor, spirit, courage, humor, force, mind, intellect, her love were gone. The reverse of *ensoulment*.

When does life begin? And end? I have been privy to see-ing both. For myself, I view each as sacred, and not for me to try to legislate even if I could. But I respect the privacy and right of someone else to decide differently.

I think of the twelve-week-old fetus in anatomy lab floating in a bottle of formaldehyde, a fetus about the size of the wooden Christ Child in the crèche we bought in Bethlehem. And of the outlines of the babies of each of our three oldest daughters as I watched them having ultrasound scans for possible problems. I thought of the very different destinies of each fetus. One of those forms miscarried at twelve weeks. No one made a whole lot of fuss. Of course, there was disappointment, but the doctor assured the mother and father that they would have more, that the fetus obviously was in trouble enough to self-abort.

For the other two, the ultrasounds came at the end of their pregnancies. Their shapes were more clear, even the sex was visible. For the baby boy, there was an easy birth, an easy first year of life in an adoring world. For the baby girl, there would be a tenuous existence in the womb, a bedside monitor for six months after birth, to give warning if the fragile heart or imperfect lungs quit in the night. I think of the precariousness of her survival. And I go cold thinking of anything that might ever have damaged her, let alone destroyed her. At the same time, I admit, I would have cared even more intensely about the fate of her mother.

Was there ever an issue to be given more thoughtful, prayerful consideration? An issue closer to our center of feeling?

Twenty-seven years ago I was happily pregnant with that fourth daughter, the one now about to have her first baby. In the playroom where her three older sisters—still little girls— were watching, I was trying to put a new lining in the old family cradle, laughing because I was so out of sorts trying to make the sides fit the pink satin. Not my line of work, and we all knew it. I'd always had two dispositions: normal, and sewing. I turned on the TV to help. To Channel 7, PBS, and ironically to the story of Margaret Sanger. The impact of that documentary has never left me. When I tuned in, Margaret, a nurse in a Brooklyn tenement around the turn of the century, was trying to save the life of a woman who had tried to abort herself with a coat hanger. Bleeding to death, the woman wept to the nurse who held her, "I tried to tell him where they came from [point-ing to what seemed like a room full of children in that sad one-room apartment], but he says I'm the only thing he has—and what could I do?"

I watched that film to the end, saw Margaret Sanger strug-gle to educate those tenement women, fight for them in court, get sanction for them to take some reasonable control of their lives before they lost them. I saw Margaret, in her willingness to love mercy, become the subject of scorn, harassment, and threats. She had to defend herself in court and on the street because she was an advocate of birth control for the poor.

All the time I poked my needle through the stiff old wicker to the soft satin of the cradle that had rocked three generations of wanted babies to well-fed sleep, thinking There but for the grace of God go I—the outrageous grace of the God I so wholly believe in as the giver of the life I love and want so much to pass along. Complicated, that giving of life, and the giving and taking of the quality of life. I never felt more humble, never more passionately wished that the grace that came to me and my happy children might also extend to all women, and all their children.

Four years later, I had a fifth baby, with complications enough that I had to have a tubal ligation after she was born, miraculously well, even beautiful, in spite of much difficulty. Demerol, the drug given me over and over for gall bladder pain that repeatedly triggered labor in the last trimester of my preg-nancy preserved her by allowing me to carry her into the eighth month of pregnancy. But it took me three agonizing months after her birth to regain myself after addiction to the drug. In spite of it all, we survived, both of us, and gained new strength as she became the family plaything, happiness for us all.

For six years of her growing up, I, as a member of the General Board of the Mormon Church's youth organization, wrote lessons and gave Standards Night talks on chastity and temple marriage, the challenges and joys of mothering. At the same time, as a part-time member of the board of Odyssey House, a drug rehabilitation center, I saw pictures of children born to prostitutes addicted to drugs not unlike the Demerol that caused me such agony. Many of these children were born addicted and sold into the sickening, burgeoning business of child pornography. I shudder now remembering pictures of those children. I wonder how it was for the mothers who bore them. For both mothers and children, the daily horror or bleakness of life with quality totally absent. Every morning each child faced such an uneven destiny that no two circumstances could possibly be equated.

And I remember the seven girls who over a period of seven years came to live in our home, "unwed mothers" from the Relief Society Social Services. From a very young seventeen to a very mature thirty-four, those young women enriched and taught us what we might never have known of sacrifice and courage as they gave their babies up for adoption and went back to their own lives impoverished by the loss of the babies they would never take home with them. Quality given, pain absorbed. The whole experience perceived by many as born of sin, but made less "sinful" because they went through with the births and gave their babies to "good homes." What might education or Margaret Sanger have helped the "unwed mothers" or those prostitute mothers to avoid?

Through the years I've watched adopted kids grow up in loving homes to be both joy and devastation for those who have wanted so much to have them. As with all kids, their growing up is seldom easy, their claim on the joy or grief of their parents no different from the claims of other children. Parenting was never all gloss and bubbles, no matter the circumstances. Giving birth cannot assure happiness for either mother or child, nor can giving that baby away.

In the past three years I've sat on a lay advisory committee to the OB/GYN department at the University of Utah Medical Center. We've heard experts talk about in vitro births, artificial insemination, methods for sustaining fragile pregnancies. We've listened to ecstatic couples who have carried babies they would earlier have lost to miscarriages.

At the same time, a year ago, I spent five weeks at an artists' colony where four of seven residents—painters, writers, composers—had chosen not to have children. These were concerned people, informed and aware of inequities, over-population, starvation, of a world that needed careful attention to its welfare. Nevertheless, they reveled in hearing every detail about my family and even smilingly put up with snapshots of them and lines from their letters. Each of us was enriched for respecting choices not our own.

Complicated indeed, this business of having babies—or not. Personal, private, often excruciating the choices, the eventualities. And who could possibly decide whose choice is what it should be? I'd hate to be the one to judge. In fact, the longer I live, the more convinced I become that it's all I can possibly handle just to try to come to grips with what besets my own life, to try to make sense of my own sense of morality. I think often of the admonishment of David O. McKay, the prophet of my growing-up years, that such decisions be the private affair of a couple and the Lord.

Two weeks ago I sat with my fifth daughter far away from home. That Sunday we were across the continent visiting in a fundamentalist church. We listened with distress and despair to the head of that church as he made blanket condemnations of "those murderers who take the life of a fetus." Women, medical people, all were collectively damned. I wondered how that judgment would feel to the frantic, pregnant woman in Margaret Sanger's arms, to Margaret Sanger. To me, who after the birth of my youngest daughter had elected to end my child-bearing potential. I lived in a world in which such a choice was mine.

I sat in that church and remembered sitting two years ago in a Teenage Pregnancy Conference at the YWCA where I was to be a speaker. Though thinking myself fairly well informed, I trembled to hear a judge, a counselor, the director of a home for pregnant adolescents, tell of thirteen-year-olds keeping their babies "for companionship" and then abusing or abandoning them because they felt sapped of their girlhood, their chance to be young and free. And at the same time hearing of fifteen-year-olds having their third and fourth abortions. Every "case" different, no two answerable to the same solution. Reverence for life? Whose life? What life?

All I could think then, pray now, is this: Dear Lord, give me the heart to understand, the wisdom not to judge, the loving kindness to know what the poet Gwendolyn Brooks meant when she wrote, "That even in my deliberateness I was not deliberate." All I could do was think that if my daughter's friend chooses a different destiny for another spina bifida child, I will love them both for their likeness to and their difference from me.

Where do I stand on abortion? On the side of life. For mother as well as child. Not bewildered by not deciding exactly where I stand except in reverencing both the life and the agency that the Lord alone gives to decide anything at all.

And I go gratefully, ecstatically, to welcome in another grandbaby of my own.

Postscript: The new little girl born April 30, 1985, in UCLA Hospital came out sucking her thumb and looking brightly at a world where her healthy seven pounds, fourteen ounces would be held like treasure, even at 3 A.M. by parents exhausted by responsibility and beaming with the chance to take it on. And Grandma Grey is home, happy as a clam—and glad to be in the stage where someone else is doing it for me: the deciding, the having, the finding out. Too tired and satisfied to want to go back a single day. Ready for this spring and whatever birthing it portends.

Note

[1] The poem "The Mother," by Gwendolyn Brooks, is from her book, *Blacks* (Chicago: Third World Press, 1991).

A PHI BETA KAPPA KEY AND
A SAFETY PIN

Commencement Address
University of Utah, 1992

IT IS CUSTOMARY FOR commencement speakers to give advice to graduates. I am going to do that in the only way historians know—by telling stories about the past. The story I want to tell is my own.

Thirty-two years ago I was one of two graduating seniors to speak at commencement. Here is how I began:

> *This is the night when university graduates look forward with high hopes to the future—that is male university graduates. The popular press won't let us women graduates forget that we face a frustrating struggle ahead, a struggle which a recent Newsweek cover depicted as the choice between a Phi Beta Kappa key and a safety pin.*

No, I wasn't a woman ahead of her time. Having raised what would be the most explosive issue of the next decade, I immediately dropped it, turning to what I thought was a more important topic. I am grateful to my alma mater for bringing me back to finish that speech.

As I stood at the podium in 1960, I epitomized the very issue I had raised. Gael and I had married during my junior year at the U. In June I received my Phi Beta Kappa key. Four months later, I got my safety pin. I gave birth to my first child in Boston where Gael had begun graduate work at the Massachusetts Institute of Technology.

Those of you raised in the age of Pampers and velcro wrappers may not immediately grasp the complex symbolism of a safety pin. In my generation, girls were raised with powerful thumbs and giving hearts. In the crucible of babysitting (or "tending" as we called it in Idaho), we learned how to push a dull pin through fourteen layers of gauze diaper without spearing the baby. That was training for an important life work—motherhood.

In 1960, it simply did not occur to me or to Gael or to anyone around us that a mother, even one who was valedictorian of her class, might also think about graduate school. I believe that one of my professors, G. Homer Durham, suggested I sign up for an interview with a representative of the Woodrow Wilson Fellowship Foundation.

"I'm having a baby," I answered lightly, and that was the end of that. The irony is that I received a Woodrow Wilson Fellowship seventeen years later when I was the mother of five children, including one rather small baby. Why, in 1960, was it unthinkable to consider combining motherhood and scholarship?

"Oh, but you were in Utah," a colleague said to me recently.

No, that wasn't the problem. In our apartment building in Cambridge, Massachusetts, in the early sixties, I was surrounded by women exactly like me. One of my closest friends had dropped out of Mt. Holyoke when she became pregnant. Another gave up her education when she snagged a senior from Brown. We women with Phi Beta Kappa keys took in sewing, baby-sat for other people's children, did part-time clerical work, while our husbands were at M.I.T., Harvard, or Brandeis.

A few weeks ago I went to the library and tracked down the March 7, 1960, issue of *Newsweek*, the one with the Phi Beta Kappa key and the safety pin on the cover. A banner headline—"Young Wives with Brains"—announced a special "science" report inside. Reading it helped me to understand why I couldn't possibly have said more about women's issues in my commencement speech. The article begins this way:

> As she pauses in front of her mirror, the thoughtful young woman
> (GENUS American Mother HABITAT Upper Income Bracket)
> can look upon a triple image unique in the history of her sex.
>
> First there is the healthy, glowing beauty, the product of good
> obstetrics, good nutrition, and good living. . . . A woman freed from
> the tyranny of her body.
>
> Then behind the casually perfect makeup, there is a mind

sharpened by sixteen years of schooling. . . . A woman freed from the tyranny of ignorance.

Thirdly, there are the fashionable clothes that proclaim a life style made possible by an industrious husband who earns $20,000 a year. A woman freed from the tyranny of poverty.

She should be pleased with herself, and yet she is not. For there is a fourth image in the glass, the image of discontent.

The author went on to suggest that college-educated women were the victims of affluence or the isolation of the suburbs or inflated expectations about sexual fulfillment. But it also invoked the Freudian dictum "anatomy is destiny," quoting the President of the National Council on Family Relations, who expressed dismay that "otherwise intelligent women" seemed "mad because their husbands cannot become pregnant and do not have to bear children and raise them." The underlying assumption, of course, was that discontented women rejected their own femininity.

Reading this essay I felt a bit like my daughter when she gets out our old yearbooks. "Oh! Look at the silly hairdos!" she exclaims. "Did people really look like that?"

"Yes," I tell her, "and thirty years from now your yearbook picture will look funny, too." The historian's job is to help people see why things look funny. We talk lightly in our society about personal choice. But choices are made in the context of enormous social pressures. Standing outside our own time, we can sometimes see that. So for a few minutes, I would like to probe the three presumed "freedoms" identified in the opening passage of that *Newsweek* article. Notice that each was based on the premise that things had never been better for women.

Let's begin with "freedom from the tyranny of the body." The article was quite right in identifying the conquest of childbed fever as one of the important events of the modern era. But scientific childbirth, which by the 1930s really was beginning to reduce maternal and infant mortality, brought a new kind of tyranny with it. Listen to this account of a modern hospital delivery about 1937. I am afraid that when I read it to you, you will think it is satire. It is not. This was the birth well-educated women in the 1940s and nearly everybody by the 1960s expected:

> [When the woman arrives at the hospital] she is immediately given the benefit of one of the modern analgesics or pain-killers. Soon she is in a dreamy, half-conscious state . . . at the height of a pain, sound asleep between spasms. . . . She knows nothing about being taken to a spotlessly clean delivery room, placed on a sterile table, draped with sterile sheets; neither does she see her attendants, the doctor and nurses, garbed for her protection in sterile white gowns and gloves; nor the shiny boiled instruments and antiseptic solutions. She does not hear the cry of her baby when first he feels the chill of this cold world, or see the care with which the doctor repairs such lacerations as may have occurred. She is, as most of us want to be when severe pain has us in its grasp—asleep. Finally she awakes in smiles, a mother with no recollection of having become one.[1]

This description is barely distinguishable from the account of delivery I read before Karl was born. As I recall, the author skirted the details of labor with the cheerful phrase, "by this time you will be floating on a pink cloud."

I was awake when Karl was born, but most of the women around me were not. I saw my son's little body and I heard his cry, but I was temporarily paralyzed from the waist down and still drowsy from medication. As hospital policy required, Gael had left me eight hours before. I gave birth among strangers, while he went home and slept. There was nothing else he could do. In the morning, he was a father with no recollection of having become one.

The medical establishment of the 1950s had forgotten what Martha Ballard, my eighteenth-century Maine midwife, knew two hundred years ago—that childbirth and in fact all healing involves the mind and spirit as well as the body. Fortunately nurse-midwives and a new generation of doctors throughout the United States are helping us reclaim that knowledge.

At this distance, the college woman's "freedom from ignorance" seems just as ironic. I am immensely grateful for the education I received at the University of Utah. I have often said that Bill Mulder was my anchor on one side of University Street and Lowell Bennion on the other. Their influence is reflected in my commencement speech, which includes quotations from nineteenth-century American literature and from the Old Testament. I argued that graduating seniors had difficulty deciding what to do with their lives because they hadn't learned "to respond emotionally as well as intellectually to an idea, to become involved in it personally and activated by it." I quoted Thoreau: "How many a man has dated a new era in his life from the reading of a book."

As I spoke those words, I was about to begin a new era in my own life, but I have to admit Thoreau wasn't a great deal of help. Imagine dropping into the chasm of motherhood with a book by a bachelor transcendentalist who lived in a solitary cabin in the woods! I actually have a photograph of myself, large with child, taken near Walden Pond in Concord, Massachusetts, on Columbus Day 1960. A couple of years later, inspired by *Walden*, I threw away my ironing board. Even in the age of polyester that was about the best I could do to become "man thinking."

Please don't misunderstand me. I believe that literature has the power to transcend boundaries of time, age, race, gender, and class. But despite the riches of my undergraduate education, there was something missing—the voices of women.

Since sixth grade I had wanted to be a writer. I used to send things off to *Seventeen* magazine and when I was eighteen I actually had something published. But the longer I spent in school, the less I was able to write. I don't think that was an accident.

In the 1950s bright women were condemned for wanting to *be* men, but in our intellectual lives we were forced to read and speak with male eyes and in male voices. Listen to me in the culminating paragraph of my graduation address: "The world needs scholars. But even more it needs men who can respond to the great issues of our time. . . . Turning our intellectual resources upon them, we may cry with another man, writing over 2500 years ago . . ." And so on. Those words sound comical today. In 1960 they were standard written English.

The 1950s were *not* a high point for women's education.

The great gains came in the nineteenth and early twentieth centuries, and in many fields there was actually a decline in female participation by 1960. Thanks to the G.I. Bill, bright young men dominated classrooms and eventually the faculties of American universities. I believe I had three female professors at the U, one of them the fearsome and mysterious Clarice Short. Even though she planted a C+ on my first paper, she made me want to be an English major. I thought she was invincible. I wept recently when I read the excerpts from her diary published after her death in *The Owl on the Aerial*. This magnificent teacher, scholar, and poet, like so many women of her generation and mine, didn't know she had anything worth saying. I am not sure which is worse, the tyranny of ignorance or the tyranny of an education.

There is a happy ending to Clarice Short's story. At the age of sixty-three at the urging of friends, she published her first book of poetry, *The Old One and the Wind*. Thanks to the women's movement's insistence on equal pay for equal work, she also got a raise. In the early seventies her salary was only two-thirds that of male professors of her same rank and workload. So much for the "freedoms from poverty" celebrated in the *Newsweek* article. That "freedom," as you will recall, depended upon marriage to an upper-income male.

From this distance it is easy to see that the three freedoms touted in the *Newsweek* story represented a particularly insidious kind of bondage, a pampered dependency that in several important areas of life denied women the ability to give as well as receive. Women could benefit from, but not create, the miracles of modern medicine. We were encouraged to learn but not teach, spend without earning. The women's movement of the 1970s was not an effort to abandon responsibility but to reclaim it. In the university, in the economy, and in the delivery room, women discovered it was better to feel pain than to suffer oblivion.

We were sustained not just by hopes for the future but by a new understanding of the past. The lives of "traditional women," women like Martha Ballard, taught us that American women had always sustained their communities as well as their homes. We also learned from women who claimed more public roles. Listen to this voice:

> It is time that we utterly repudiate the pernicious dogma that mar-
> riage and a practical life-work are incompatible.[2]

Radical 1970s feminist? No, this is Louisa Greene Richards, a pious Latter-day Saint mother writing in the *Woman's Exponent,* published in the territory of Utah in 1877. I *can* date a new era in my life from reading such words.

I am grateful that thirty-two years ago, I earned both a Phi Beta Kappa key and a safety pin and that for the past twenty years I have been able to combine motherhood with "a practical life-work." My children's lives have been enriched by my scholarship, and my scholarship has been enriched by my life as a housewife and mother. When people ask me how I have done it, I usually say, "A little at a time." It took me five years to complete a one-year M.A., nine to do a Ph.D., eight years to write Martha Ballard's book.

Meanwhile Gael and I *together* raised our children. Louisa Greene Richards had something to say about that as well:

> No woman worthily and happily married is less fitted to aid the
> general progress of the world than she who stands alone with none
> to hinder; yes, with none to hinder, but with none to help her either,
> in the exercise of her best gifts.[3]

Even more important than the practical help Gael offered, and there was a lot of that, was his faith in me. He believed in my best gifts, even when I did not. So, if I have any wish for you today, it is that you will discover your best gifts and be blessed with a companion who will help you use them. Thirty years from now, some things about today will look funny, but the best things—the gifts of the mind and the spirit—will endure.

In 1965 Clarice Short sat in a room in Cambridge, Massachusetts, writing in her diary and thinking about her own past. She wrote: "The years close up like a fan bringing widely separated events together into a state beyond time."[4]

I hope that by folding my past against your present, I have given you the courage to make your own history.

Notes

[1] Quoted in Judith Walzer Leavitt, *Brought to Bed,: Childbearing in America, 1750-1950* (New York: Oxford University Press, 1986), pp. 180–181.

[2] Louisa Greene Richard, *Woman's Exponent,* August 15, 1877, in Susan Kohler, "Woman's Exponent Revisited," *Exponent II*, October 1974, p. 8.

[3] Ibid.

[4] Clarice Short, *The Owl on the Aerial,* ed. Barbara J. Durree, (Salt Lake City: Signature Books, 1990), p. 110.

LANDSCAPES OF THE MIND

I KNEW TED BUNDY. And I've been thinking about him and pictures and mountains.

He was an investigator of Mormonism at a university student ward where my husband was bishop. In 1974 we saw him often. He was an attractive, convivial law student living away from his home state of Washington, and as we did with others, we invited him to Sunday dinner—three times. Each time he was unable to come, but commented to my husband about how good looking our daughters were. We had five, four of them teenagers, two with long brown hair parted in the middle—as did each of the eight girls he assaulted and killed not far from where we chatted those days at the church across from the campus under the mountains.

In his last hours, across the continent in Florida and after ten years of thwarted attempts at reprieve, Ted Bundy did his confessing. Part of it was a half-hour videotaped interview on the influence of pornography, about the horrors he had indulged, the alcohol he said he consumed to make him less inhibited, more able. We watched, heard the whole thing. It was more than unsettling. This was no case study. He had sat next to me in a chapel, served me as a waiter at a festive ward party. Over those weeks, I had introduced him to girls, and we all had talked. In the interview, he said that at that time in Salt Lake City his mind was churning with the compulsions and filth which he claimed eventually claimed him. While evidence suggested that he never hurt anyone he knew—his victims were strangers, innocents—the fact of my knowing him gave an eerie gloss to his articulate, emotional but controlled informing, like a night illuminated by the scariest lightning.

He was the boy next door, consumed by the consumption of what I had resisted fighting formally, the availability to children of what he said would never have been shown even in an X-rated movie house thirty years ago. Of course, my believing him was tempered by knowing his ability to manipulate his voracious public. When had he ever told the truth? And of course, such aberrant behavior as his *had* to be triggered by more than exposure to pornography, even the grotesque, sex-exploiting violence that he said he needed more and more of. But something in me believed him this time. I was sickened—and afraid. I thought with new explicitness of young heads that absorb and then psyches that act on what is there.

I thought of growing up with a mother who believed that "little minds need to be filled with good thoughts." She had my three brothers and me spend days cutting out our favorite pictures from the *Saturday Evening Post*, Norman Rockwell and the Campbell Kiddies. Sometimes we even had a *National Geographic* with exotic natives or polar bears. With paste made of flour and water and a pinch of sugar, we'd paste them into scrapbooks to look at for years, or she'd glue them to the calsomined wood wall of the cabin. There they stuck between our natural curiosities and childhood experimentings. Radios supplied our images by ear, and characters in books were imagined, based whimsically on what we went to sleep and woke up to—boy scouts and flags and Indians in canoes on a tranquil river, a puzzled lover kneeling before twin ladies trying to decide which would get his bouquet.

And there were mountains, sturdy and holding, not only all around us, but in lots of those pictures rumpling on their pages or walls. A collage of some favorites still lives above the balcony of the cabin we now go to with those five daughters, their husbands, and a new generation of children whose minds are never *not* being fed something.

I thought of those grandchildren, of course. All of them, born blessedly whole and in homes where they're cared for, have a chance of growing up as Ted did, OK on the outside. But what do television "blood and guts" and the grotesque caricatures of "Garbage Pail Kids" cards exchanged like we did baseball cards—in anything but secret on school playgrounds—promise to feed into those insides? And heavy metal, half-dressed "romantic themes" on MTV in the afternoon? It's a crazy world of information at some levels, way beyond the ken of two six-year-old cousins who in the car were comparing adventures—just as we used to do with our cousins, but not in front of adults, you can be sure. Coulson: "I have a girlfriend." Michael: "I have ten." Coulson: "I've kissed my girlfriend." Michael: "Did you French kiss?" Coulson: "No, but I know how."

What they had was maybe the little knowledge that Mr. Garrett in Biology told us was a dangerous thing. What does that portend for a nine-year-old naively composing a song with words she had no way of understanding: "I've gotta have your bod!" Where will she and those six-year-olds be at sixteen? What will they have seen, learned "how" about?

A social worker friend says that MTV was systematically turned off in rehab centers—and that kids thanked the counselors. But how does one cultivate appropriate guidelines in a world inundated by poison? So much is so good, so tasty as well as tasteful and, yes, uplifting as well as entertaining.

I think of how easy it is to pull up on this computer screen anything I've put into the system—hundreds of files, millions of words with a touch on the keyboard. Or how, in the far more complex and refined system inside my head, I can, like a magnificent slide projector, flash shapes, colors, scenes, ideas, faces, acts, everything I've ever let in, by or against my will, full color and life-size. To react to. Like the way my secret love strolled down the hall to his locker at Irving Jr. High. Or the sound of wind on a loose tent flap, or the taste of Mother's crusty hot bread spread with butter and chili sauce, or the feel of a newborn's cheek against mine, or the smell of newly dug earth. Or maggots in the decaying insides of my kitten that out of love and curiosity I dug up when I was eight from its five-day-old grave in the yard.

Somewhere in there, I have stored it all for later consumption.

Like Emerson, I can't remember the books I've read any more than the meals I've eaten; even so, they have made me. Mountains, books, smells, tastes, feelings, views—Theodore Bundy, I never felt more aware of the power you have over me. And I never felt more impelled to direct in some positive way the diet of what gets to have that power.

But how? Certainly I want *not* to move toward the insidious imposition of "official" opinion about what is harmful, yes, even in my eyes evil, as consumption for those I love and those I will never know. As an adult, I want a lot of choice—and my own sense of what I choose to be up for thoughtful discrimination.

And no, I don't want prudery to select our library books. I remember too well smiling with stack card in hand when, as a senior at the university, I was at last eligible to prowl the reserved shelves for Boccaccio or Lawrence or check out Macgoon's *Love and Marriage*. This when I also chose and was assigned lots else that breathed the fresh or stale and some-times stiff stuff that made up the hodgepodge of adventure, history, beauty, heroes and heroines—excellence—into my young and very inquisitive, often lazy mind. Those were the days of a sort of willingness to be led and fed that typified my growing up. Who can be unrealistic enough to expect to return to the protected post-Depression days of sweetness and light when even to say the word "pregnant" instead of "expecting" was pretty racy?

But realism and sadism need to be differentiated just as sewage must be from drinking water. The difference can be excruciatingly apparent even to the most naive. As a lay person on a committee in the 70s for Odyssey House, a drug rehabili-tation center, I saw and retained what I would love to be rid of. In my brain are indelibly stamped the sickening images of child pornography, worse than any of a kitten five days buried. They were passed out as impetus for us to mount a campaign among our legislators against alcoholism and drug addiction through the sale of milk-based drinks to the untapped market of women under forty and children. Not only women, but their children became the victims of their own addictions, to be sold and pho-tographed, used as diseased entertainment for minds that might be filled with little else. It was like being involved with mental disorder; once you've been associated with it, you will never have another doubt as to its exquisite delineations. I knew that what I was seeing was pornographic. I try not to see it still. And the best way is to fill my mind with better things to bring up.

So I didn't watch—no halo for me, I just couldn't stand to—I only read about the response in Florida to Bundy's execution, far more revolting than even the electrocution of a deranged and dangerous human being. Hucksters with T-shirts and souveneir menus gleefully touting "FRY!" detailed drawings of "Old Sparky," thirty-six select witnesses, and hundreds gathered like heated Madam DeFarges at the guillotine to cheer the hearse as it left the prison. This was a *person* being killed—even if he was a person who probably deserved anything the state might impose.

But how much of that response was let loose by the very exposure to violence that the death penalty is supposed to deter? Was the death of this man an invitation to indulge our basest inclinings? And what might a diet of such invitations do to corrode our sensibilities and temper our indignation at the horrible?

Is there any chance for balancing that gross input? At least among those who might be most exploited—women and children? Might there be offered, in fact insisted on, a modern fare of Mother's kind of feeding? I don't expect Norman Rockwell to ride the airwaves or *National Geographic* to supply the excitement of *Miami Vice,* soaps, or NFL football. But how about an urgent attempt at balance—the enriching stuff being made as broadly available as the ugly? The yukkiest yuk not mailable or living room available? The sleaziest banned somehow despite the increasing appetite of the American viewer for more and more?

Of course, I'm a dreamer. I can't have much to say about what happens in the world at large. But I hope that in my own world I can have plenty to say about the images that I let in. I'm not naive enough to suppose that my grandchildren will not see lots and lots that I was spared in my protected growing up. Nor, I think, would I want them to be narrowed down by close-minded brainwashing by even the best intended.

But there is a difference between prudishness and prudence. And I can't help wishing for every child, every adult, the privilege of great doses of light and gentleness for every swallowing of murk and cruelty. And this has to do with more than what eyes bring into brains from any screen or page. It calls for antivenom—kindness and reverence for life, shots of love and open affection, medication of quality, nonpablum entertainment, and stirrings in of sweetness and the green the earth has to offer.

After a battering of the muck, I need my mountains to restore my sense and senses. I'd love to see those mountains on every screen out there to say that Ted Bundy's horrors are only a fraction of the picture. In *The Tangled Wing*, biologist Melvin Kemper describes how the mind lights up the brain. And I'm praying that the landscapes of the mind, any mind that I might have anything to do with, might be lighted by images that also involve the soul, too lovely to be blotted out by the horrors that played on the lives of Ted Bundy and those not lucky enough to have a choice.

LUSTERWARE

I HAVE BEEN THINKING lately about an Emily Dickinson poem I first heard twenty-five years ago in an American literature class at the University of Utah. I remember feeling intrigued and somewhat troubled as the professor read the poem, since he was reported to be a lapsed Mormon. "Was that how it felt to lose faith?" I thought.

> It dropped so low—in my Regard—
> I heard it hit the Ground—
> And go to pieces on the Stones
> At bottom of my Mind—
> Yet blamed the Fate that flung it—less
> Than I denounced Myself,
> For entertaining Plated Wares
> Upon my Silver Shelf—

Since then I have lost faith in many things, among them Olympia typewriters, *New York Times* book reviews, and texturized vegetable protein; and yes, like most Latter-day Saints I have had to reconsider some of my deepest religious beliefs. I have always been a somewhat skeptical person. I can remember raising my arm in Beehive class in the Sugar City Ward and telling my teacher that regardless of what she said I did *not* think polygamy was sent by God. That kind of behavior may have had something to do with the palm reading I received from another teacher at an MIA gypsy party. She traced the lines on my upturned hand and told me my "head" line was longer and better developed than my "heart" line. For a while I worried about that.

As I have grown older, I have become less fearful of those "stones at the bottom of my mind." In fact, I am convinced that a willingness to admit disbelief is often essential to spiritual growth. All of us meet challenges to our faith—persons who fail to measure up, doctrines that refuse to settle comfortably

into our minds, books that contain troubling ideas or disorient-
ing information. The temptation is strong to "Blame the fate
that flung it" or to ignore the crash as it hits the ground, pretending that nothing has changed. Neither technique is very
useful. Though a few people seem to have been blessed with
foam rubber rather than stones at the bottom of their minds
(may they rest in peace), sooner or later most of us are forced
to confront our shattered beliefs.

I find Emily Dickinson's little poem helpful. Some things
fall off the shelf because they did not belong there in the first
place; they were "Plated Wares" rather than genuine silver. At
first I didn't fully grasp the image. The only "Plated Wares" I
knew anything about were made by Oneida or Wm. Rogers.
Although less valuable than sterling, that sort of silverplate
hardly falls to pieces when dropped. Then I learned about lusterware, the most popular "Plated Wares" of Emily Dickinson's
time. In the late eighteenth century, British manufacturers
developed a technique for decorating ceramic ware with a gold
or platinum film. In one variety, a platinum luster was applied
to the entire surface of the object to produce what contempo-
raries called "poor man's silver." Shiny, inexpensive, and easy to
get, it was also fragile, as breakable as any other piece of pottery or china. Only a gullible or very inexperienced person
would mistake it for true silver.

All of us have lusterware as well as silver on that shelf we
keep at the top of our minds. A lusterware Joseph Smith, for
instance, is unfailingly young, handsome, and spiritually radiant; unschooled but never superstitious, persecuted but never
vengeful, human but never mistaken. A lusterware image fulfills
our need for an ideal without demanding a great deal from us.
There are lusterware missions and marriages, lusterware friend-
ships, lusterware histories, and yes, lusterware visions of ourselves. Most of these will be tested at some point on the stones
at the bottom of our minds.

A number of years ago I read a letter from a young woman
who had recently discovered some lusterware on her own
shelf. "I used to think of the Church as one hundred percent
true," she wrote. "But now I realize it is probably ten percent

human and only ninety percent divine." I gasped, wanting to write back immediately, "If you find any earthly institution that is *ten percent* divine, embrace it with all your heart!" Actually ten percent is probably too high an estimate. Jesus spoke of grains of salt and bits of leaven, and he told his disciples that "the kingdom of heaven is like unto treasure hid in a field; the which when a man hath found, he hideth, and for joy thereof goeth and selleth all that he hath, and buyeth that field" (Matt. 13:44). Thus a small speck of divinity—the salt in the earth, the leaven in the lump of dough, the treasure hidden in the field—gives value and life to the whole. Now the question is, where in The Church of Jesus Christ of Latter-day Saints do we go to find the leaven: To the bishop? To the prophet? To the lesson manuals? Do we find it in Relief Society? In sacrament meeting? And if we fail to discover it in any of these places shall we declare the lump worthless? Jesus' answer was clear. The leaven must be found in one's own heart or not at all: "the kingdom of God is within you" (Luke 17:21).

Many years ago a blunt bishop countered one of my earnest complaints with a statement I have never forgotten: "The Church is a good place to practice the Christian virtues of forgiveness, mercy, and love unfeigned." That was a revelation to me. The Church was not a place that exemplified Christian virtues so much as a place that required them. I suppose I had always thought of it as a nice cushion, a source of warmth and comfort if ever things got tough (which they seldom had to that point in my life). It hadn't occurred to me that the Church could *make* things tough.

Eliza R. Snow expressed it this way in a hymn that seems to be missing from the new book:

Think not when you gather to Zion,
Your troubles and trials are through,
That nothing but comfort and pleasure
Are waiting in Zion for you:
No, no, 'tis designed as a furnace,
All substance, all textures to try,
To burn all the "wood, hay, and stubble,"
The gold from the dross purify.

Probably the hymn deserved to be dropped from the book. The third stanza suggests that the author, like more than one Relief Society president since, had made too many welfare visits and had listened to too many sad stories. Her charity failing, she told the complainers in her ward to shape up and solve their own problems:

> *Think not when you gather to Zion,*
> *The Saints here have nothing to do*
> *But to look to your personal welfare,*
> *And always be comforting you.*

In the Church, as in your own families, we have the worst and the best of times.

A young missionary on a lonely bus ride somewhere in Bolivia thinks he is equal to what lies ahead. He can endure hard work, strange food, and a confusing dialect. But nothing in the Mission Training Center has prepared him for the filthiness of the apartment, for the cynicism of his first companion, or for the parakeet who lives, with all its droppings, under the other young man's bed.

A young bride, ready to enter the temple, feels herself spiritually prepared. By choosing a simple white gown usable later as a temple dress she has already shown her preference for religious commitment over fantasy. She has discussed the covenants with her stake president and she feels she understands them. Yet sitting in the endowment room in ritual clothing no one had thought to show her, saying words she does not understand, she turns to her mother in dismay. "Am I supposed to enjoy this?" she says.

An elders quorum president, pleased that his firm has won the contract for the ward remodeling project, prepares for the hard work ahead. He knows the job will be demanding. He expects some tension between his responsibilities as a project manager and his commitment to the Church, but he is ready to consecrate his time and talents for the building up of the Kingdom. What he doesn't expect is the anger and the humiliation that follow his year-long encounter with the Church bureaucracy. "I wonder how far up this sort of thing goes?" he asks and contemplates leaving the Church.

A middle-aged woman reads deeply in the scriptures, sharing her insights with friends individually and in a small study group. She feels secure in her quest for greater light and truth until she begins to examine certain troubling episodes in Church history. The discrepancy between the official accounts and the new accounts distresses her. Has she been lied to? And if in one issue, why not many? Confiding her doubts to her friends, she feels them back away.

"And the rain descended, and the floods came, and the winds blew, and beat upon that house; and it fell not: for it was founded upon a rock" (Matt. 7:25). What rock can secure us against such storms? Occasionally some gentle soul, perhaps as puzzled as my Beehive teacher by my outspoken ways, will ask, "What keeps you in the Church?" "My skepticism," I answer, only half in jest. Over the years I have noticed that Saints with doubts often outlast "true believers." But of course the answer is inadequate. I don't stay in the Church because of what I don't know, but because of what I do.

The Church I believe in is not an ascending hierarchy of the holy. It is millions of ordinary people calling one another "brother" and "sister" and trying to make it true. Not so long ago I had one of those terrible-wonderful experiences that I have been talking about. It started in an innocuous way, then built to a genuine crisis, a classic Liahona-Iron Rod conflict between me and my bishop. After a week of sleepless nights, I went into his office feeling threatened and fragile. What followed was an astonishingly open and healing discussion, a small miracle. As I told a friend later, "If we hadn't been Mormons, we would have embraced!" Our opinions didn't change much; our attitudes toward one another did. I give him credit for having the humility to listen, and I give myself credit for trusting him enough to say what I really felt. The leaven in our lump was a common reaching for the Spirit.

I am not always comfortable in my ward. There are weeks when I wonder if I can sit through another Relief Society lesson delivered straight from the manual or endure another meandering discussion in Gospel Doctrine class. Yet there are also moments when, surprised by my own silence, I am able to hear what a speaker only half says. Several months ago as I was bracing myself for a fast and testimony meeting, a member of the bishopric approached me and asked if I would give the closing prayer. I said, "Yes," feeling like a hypocrite, yet at the same time silently accepting some responsibility for the success of the meeting. Were the testimonies really better? When I stood to pray, I was moved to the point of tears.

For me the issue is not whether The Church of Jesus Christ of Latter-day Saints is the One True Church Upon the Face of the Earth. That sounds to me like a particularly Zoramite brand of lusterware:

> Now the place was called by them Rameumptom, which, being interpreted, is the holy stand. Now, from this stand they did offer up, every man, the selfsame prayer. . . . We thank thee, O God, for we are a chosen people unto thee, while others shall perish. (Alma 31:21–22, 28)

The really crucial issue for me is that the Spirit of Christ is alive in the Church and that it continues to touch and redeem the lives of the individual members. The young man survived his mission, returning with a stronger, more sober sense of what it meant to serve. The bride returned to the temple and enjoyed it more. The elders quorum president, though still struggling with his anger, knows it is his problem to face and to solve. The middle-aged woman grew through her loss of faith into a richer, deeper spirituality.

As I study the scriptures, very few contemporary problems seem new. I wonder how men in tune with the divine can appear to be so complacent and self-righteous in their dealings with women. Then I read Luke's account of the visit of the angel to the women at the tomb on the first day of the week: "It was Mary Magdalene, and Joanna, and Mary the mother of James, and other women that were with them, which told these things unto the apostles. And their words seemed to them as idle tales, and they believed them not" (Luke 24:10–11). I wonder how a church purportedly devoted to eternal values can invest so much energy in issues that strike me as unimportant.

170

Then I read the nineteenth chapter of Leviticus and find the second greatest commandment, "thou shalt love thy neighbour as thyself," side by side with a sober command that "neither shall a garment mingled of linen and woollen come upon thee" (vv. 18–19). Every dispensation has had its silver and its lusterware. God speaks to his children, as Moroni taught us, in our own language and in our own narrow and culture-bound condition.

To me that is a cause for joy rather than cynicism. I love Joseph Smith's ecstatic recital in Doctrine and Covenants 128:19–21.

> Now, what do we hear in the gospel which we have received? A voice of gladness! A voice of mercy from heaven; and a voice of truth out of the earth. . . .
>
> A voice of the Lord in the wilderness of Fayette, Seneca county. . . . The voice of Michael on the banks of the Susquehanna. . . . The voice of Peter, James, and John in the wilderness between Harmony, Susquehanna county, and Colesville, Broome county . . .
>
> And again, the voice of God in the chamber of old Father Whitmer, in Fayette, Seneca county, and at sundry times, and in divers places through all the travels and tribulations of this Church of Jesus Christ of Latter-day Saints!

Joseph's litany of homely place names, his insistence that the voice of God could indeed be heard on the banks of an ordinary American river or in the chamber of a common farmer, gives his message an audacity and a power that cannot be ignored. For me Joseph Smith's witness that the divine can strike through the immediate is more important than any of the particulars enshrined in the church he established. If other people want to reduce D&C 128 to a data processing program for handling family group sheets, that's fine. What feeds my soul is knowing about that "whole and complete and perfect union, and welding together of dispensations" that Joseph wrote about.

Two or three years ago I attended a small unofficial women's conference in Nauvoo. The ostensible purpose was to celebrate the founding of the Relief Society, but the real agenda was to come to terms with the position of women in the contemporary Church. The participants came from many places, a few of us known to each other, many of us strangers, the only common bond being some connection with the five organizers, all of whom remained maddeningly opaque as to their motives. I cannot describe what happened to me during those three days. Let me just say that after emptying myself of any hope for peace and change in the Church, I heard the voice of the Lord on the banks of the Mississippi River. It was a voice of gladness, telling me that the gospel had indeed been restored. It was a voice of truth, assuring me that my concerns were just, that much was still amiss in the Church. It was a voice of mercy, giving me the courage to continue my uneasy dialogue between doubt and faith. I am not talking here about a literal voice but about an infusion of the Spirit, a kind of Pentecost that for a moment dissolved the boundaries between heaven and earth and between present and past. I felt as though I were re-experiencing the events the early Saints had described.

I am not a mystical person. In ordinary decisions in my family I am far more likely to call for a vote than a prayer, and when other people proclaim their "spiritual experiences" I am generally cautious. But I would gladly sift through a great trough of meal for even a little bit of that leaven.

The temptations of skepticism are real. Sweeping up the fragments of broken lusterware, we sometimes forget to polish and cherish the silver, not knowing that the power of discernment is one of the gifts of the Spirit, that the ability to discover counterfeit wares also gives us the power to recognize the genuine.

Emma Lou Thayne • 1986

MODELS AND HEROES

TODAY I PLAYED TENNIS in a foursome with Ednah Wood, seventy-nine. Fifty years ago she was the champion of Chile, where her geologist husband had taken the family of four for sixteen years. Fifteen years ago, widowed and retired from her position of Assistant Registrar at the University of Utah, she had a massive heart attack as she was driving away from the very courts that we played on today. No one thought she would recover, let alone play tennis again. But there she was, as she has been since the barest beginnings of her recovery, running for drop shots, quick as a cobra at the net, placing lobs and crosscourts exactly out of reach of her smiling opponents.

Who could help but smile? For every one of us who play with her each week, Ednah is a sturdy white-haired hero. She is doing what practically no other woman of my mother's generation ever did—run, run after a ball, laughing and snapping her fingers when she gets to it and puts it past the rest of us. I want to be like Ednah. She is my physical role model.

Heroes, heroines, role models—whatever, I've had dozens along the way. At least twenty years ago, I wrote an article in which I declared my allegiance to people to look to, to emulate, and then finally, most of the time, to move on from, never forgetting what they have contributed but needing something else for another stage or phase. A young wife and mother then, teaching part-time at the university, writing in corners of nights, I needed a world peopled with inspiration.

But my hero-worshipping did not start there. It began early with Whizzer White (now Justice of the Supreme Court). When I was four, my uncle lifted me up in a packed University of Utah stadium to see Whizzer run ninety-one yards for a Colorado touchdown. For years afterward, I tried broken field running while playing "Kick the Can" and "Run Sheepie Run" with my brothers and the neighborhood kids.

When I learned to read, Helen Keller was my idol. I could not read enough of or about Louisa May Alcott, because Jo in *Little Women* was everything that I could ever imagine wanting to be. Then it was Florence Nightingale. After taking their temperatures and giving shots to all sixteen dolls in the playroom, I carried my nurse's kit and wore my Red Cross uniform to bed every night. By junior high, Deanna Durbin and Judy Garland were singing on the screens at the wardhouse and at the Southeast Theater. My age exactly, they made being a leading lady look effortless and singing seem like a simple lure for stardom and first kisses.

It wasn't until high school that real people in my real world took over as models of much. Until then, my parents and brothers were too often taken for granted. Even my grandmother, who shared her bed with me, would have to wait years until I realized what an influence she had been. And sometimes it's hard to recognize a friend as a hero. But at East High there were the girls from Bryant and Roosevelt, sophisticated and chic compared to us few bumpkin mavericks from Irving. They wore lipstick—purple—and huaraches and saddle shoes. They collected in easy groups with boys who were equally suave. When they became my friends in class, the luster dimmed, and I moved comfortably with them in most situations. But I was never quite ready for the modeling ramps and cheerleading that they took to as if they were deer on a mountain.

When I entered the university, real live older "women" like Ruth Jacobson (Kirby), Christy Wicker (Freed), and Elaine Anderson (Cannon) entered my life, members of Mortar Board, student body officers, editors, beauty queens—just plain fancy coeds. And I, a very green sixteen-year-old freshman, gawked and grinned. Much later I recognized that role models had to be much more than simply the socially adept. I discovered as I became friends with Ruth, Christy, and Elaine that they were also bright, talented, solid, and thoughtful.

But college did bring my first honest-to-goodness hero: Dr. Lowell L. Bennion, director of the LDS Institute of Religion, who would alter my life for a lifetime. Much as I liked other professors, it was Dr. Bennion with his informed and loving candor, his wide humanitarianism and believing, who became my spiritual and intellectual hero.

Since then, I've never been without heroes—plural, all kinds, from generations and genders, younger, older, my own age. Someone whom I've known for a long time can suddenly emerge as a marvel in the face of tragedy; others whom I've barely met become delights in frolic. Mostly they're people I learn from. Lots. Lately I've found a new source for heroes—funerals. Last week it was one of my mother's dearest friends. She died at eighty-five after ten years of battling Alzheimer's disease, fading in and out of reality and service even as she drifted into an almost waxen face and carriage. As a speaker at her funeral, I needed to know what to talk about.

I found some very old scrapbooks of Mother's in which Mary came up from cards and notes and dim photos. I let my memory range about on the street where we were neighbors so long ago. In remembering, I went to Primary in Highland Park Ward where Mother and Mary taught together. I felt the old neighborhood clatter and pound and whisper like wind about me. In it all, Mary came alive and touched me with a quieter time: her rolls steaming on our breadboard, her hemstitching bordering my trousseau, her slender goodness giggling in our front room with her friend, my mother. Her life took on the perspective of four decades as her children grew up, married, had their own children, who then had theirs. She moved in and out of Church jobs, to this house and that, following her husband's fortunes. I was drawn to profound respect for one human life. She became my friend as well as my mother's. And my domestic hero.

That seems to be how heroes work best for me—as parts of a whole. Right now some of my heroes are: for fitness of body and soul, my daughters after pregnancy; for spirit, Camilla Kimball after the death of her Spencer; for a playful heart, Ednah Wood after cardiac surgery; for spunk and patience, my neighbors with their seven young children; friend after friend for courage and sustenance as well as for laughter and the right to bear each other along. And for indomitability and open arms, it's some Russian women I met in their motherland.

More than anything, as I grow older, I find myself in awe of those who retain their sense of self enough to be themselves, acting out of curiosity and the search for truth, not out of fear. When seven astronauts disappeared in a white cloud, I sent with them my respect for the adventurous spirit rooted in the well-grounded life. I mourn for them, even as I am glad in my heart, mind, and soul that they were, and are there to be revered. Christa McAuliffe and Judith Resnik inspire me, as do the men who were on that space shuttle. They are my heroes. Even the way I would address them goes far beyond semantics.

We are in a new place. My women poet friends are "poets" not "poetesses," any more than they might be "teacheresses" instead of "teachers." What I admire transcends considerations like sex or position; I admire the Whizzer Whites and the Lowell Bennions, the men in my family, the men with whom I work and associate. Few would dream how I feel about them.

Now watching our children grow into families of their own, I respect inordinately parents who give themselves to pleasant parenting. They represent to me the epitome of unselfishness and accomplishment. Even more, I admire single parents, who have to do it all alone, as well as women single or married who get up every morning, earn their own way, and still make home a place of sustenance. I stand in awe of people who respect themselves enough to live both in and out of their homes to "the full measure of their creation."

Like Ednah Wood, my Aunt Edna Heiner, eighty-nine, is a woman who works with affection and enjoys every step of the process. What many work years to achieve, she has always had—self-forgetfulness—as she has become a pillar to her enormous extended family. She has accepted what she didn't get to choose, is strong enough to choose what she could be. Married at seventeen, she raised five children, managed life with a husband "predisposed to drink," rode the bus at eight and six for fifty-two years to sell men's suits in the ZCMI bargain basement. But she remains her own person. An artist with afghans and quilts, she plays in the big harmonica band at the Senior Citizen's Center, laughs with us, cheers for her teams, and loves gardens, balloons, and scriptures.

She epitomizes what I cherish in my most consistent and sought out Guide, the One I pray to at night and listen to in the morning.

As I move into still another stage, I know that new heroes and old will usher me through whatever comes, like my intrepid husband who takes on our stages, changes, ailments, and arrivals with minimal complaint and always with love. Thank goodness for all of them and for the goodness they've offered me.

Laurel Thatcher Ulrich • 1987

GRACE UNDER PRESSURE

IT HAD BEEN ONE OF those Saturdays. Picking up our dog Idaho at the vet's had taken half the morning. Now I had to drive Amy to Portsmouth to her Merrie Miss meeting. I would have an hour's wait in Portsmouth, time to do a few errands, but not enough to accomplish all I had planned for the day. I dashed to the grocery store then back to the church, hoping Amy would agree to one more stop on the way home.

I had brought along a scrap of carpet and a cushion from my old sofa thinking that I might find a piece of fabric to make some throw pillows. Sew-fisticated Fabrics has first-quality drapery remnants for $2.99 a yard, and I thought I might find just the right thing. My sofa is almost as old as our dog and nearly as decrepit. Even when it was new, the cushions tended to slide off onto the floor when someone stood up; age had made the problem worse.

I headed for the fabric store with renovation in mind, Amy following behind. Maybe with a little fabric glue and some velcro I could keep those cushions where they belonged.

It took me about fifteen minutes to find $10.00 worth of fabric and notions. Figuring that I had postponed the $600 cost of a new couch, I moved toward the check-out counter in high spirits. Amy had $2.00 worth of fake fur and satin for her doll. I had half-sensed a certain frenzy at the counter as I was sorting through the draperies, but somehow it hadn't registered how truly desperate the situation was. There were at least seven women lined up ahead of me and three or four others circling in the aisles nearby.

"I don't know what happened to the other girl," said the blonde behind the counter. "She was supposed to be here at two." The poor woman was cutting 1/2 yard lengths for a quilt-maker and trying to keep her good humor. I quickly assessed the bolts of linen, lace, and calico in the line before me. Was it worth the wait? Probably not. Yet, for some reason, I settled my weight onto one hip, balanced my bolt of drapery at an easy angle, and sent Amy to the car to entertain the dog.

I am still not sure why I stayed. Maybe it had something to do with the fact that I had been writing about women's work in the eighteenth century. Poring over the most trivial details of American life, I began to pay more attention to ordinary things around me. Loading the washing machine took on a new significance. Picking up milk and eggs on the way to the vet, I thought of women whose very survival depended upon the health of their cows and hens. Normally, I will do almost anything to avoid standing in line, but that day I opened my eyes to what was around me and settled in.

I soon forgot my impatience in sheer fascination with the performance. The woman behind the counter moved like a dancer—or a traffic cop in the middle of a busy intersection. She pivoted gracefully from cash register to counter to the shelves behind her, her hands never still, her eyes never abandoning her customers. In the twenty or twenty-five minutes that I stood there, she measured and cut fabric from fourteen bolts; computed the prices of a dozen trimmings and notions; advised customers on fabric selection, yardages, and construction; directed people to other corners of the store; answered one telephone call; made two others (trying to locate the missing helper); and all the while carried on a lighthearted banter that turned our impatience first into sympathy and then into admiration.

When a tall woman asked if the by-the-yard quilt batting had to be measured at the counter, she said, "Not today." Then she told her how to measure a length by stretching her arms out like a telephone pole. "I don't care how long your arms are," she said. "Whatever they measure is a yard." The woman laughed and set about her task, her very long arms stretching off six "yards" of batting. The store may have lost a dollar or two on batting, but it didn't lose any customers.

I was especially struck with the patience the harried clerk showed with one neatly dressed, elderly woman who was buying brown fabric to cover a footstool. "Is this strong enough to withstand the cat's scratching?" she asked. Instead of hurrying her along (her entire purchase couldn't have amounted to more than $3.00), the clerk suggested that she check the poplin in another part of the store, and when she brought it back, she patiently explained the difference and helped her make the selection.

It was the woman's amazing ability to do three things at once that allowed her to give that kind of attention. She wrote yardages and prices on a separate pad of paper for each customer, entering each into the cash register when the entire list was complete. Hence, she could ring up four bags of pillow stuffing for one customer while waiting for another to find matching thread. Even while she was on the telephone, she reeled off lengths of cloth and wrote on her little pad.

"Hello, this is Suzanne at the shop. Do you know what time Ann was supposed to be here? There are about 10,000 people in the store, and it's getting a little crazy. No, don't bother Doris. I know she hasn't been feeling well. I'm sure Ann will be here soon." Her knowing grimace let us share her frustration, though her voice never lost its musical good humor.

Suzanne was a small woman, perhaps in her middle thirties, with pink nail polish and shoulder-length hair frosted in several shades of blonde. One rakish curl extended six inches below the rest. "Do you still do hair?" another customer asked. "Not anymore," she answered. Probably it was hairdressing that had taught her how to keep her hands moving while carrying on that comfortable chatter. Watching her tuck the telephone receiver between her shoulder and her chin, I thought of all those other "ordinary" women—secretaries, waitresses, day-care workers, housewives, and mothers of pre-school children—who so gracefully do three things at once.

Somewhere Suzanne had learned to sew. She answered questions quickly and with confidence. "Yes, lining is definitely a good idea," she told the woman who was making white linen slacks. "Unless you want to show off your underwear, but if you're like me, you never have underwear worth showing!" The customer laughed, then told about the time that she had worn hot pink underpants to work under her unlined slacks. Suzanne enjoyed the joke while checking the conversion chart to find out how much 36" fabric would be needed to line 42" linen.

As I watched, I marveled at the sheer intelligence at work. Seemingly without effort, Suzanne refolded and pinned each bolt as she finished cutting, keeping each customer's orders separate even though she was simultaneously waiting on three or four. Her sensitivity to people was equally impressive. She treated each woman as though her purchase really mattered. "Doing crafts?" she asked as I presented Amy's little pile of pearls and fake fur. By entering into her customer's concerns, she invited our participation in hers, transforming what could have been a miserable half-hour into a shared adventure.

Recently I read about a therapist who prescribes standing in line as a cure for Type A behavior. It's a kind of exercise, like doing leg lifts with weights hanging from the ends of the toes, awkward and uncomfortable at first, but good for strengthening weak muscles. I think he has a point. In my eagerness to get things done, I sometimes flail around like my dog when she's trapped in the back of the car, sealing off the world with my panting.

The unexpected traffic jam in the fabric store gave me a chance to try a different way. I never did get around to making new cushions for my sofa, but when I left the store some part of me had been renovated.

Emma Lou Thayne • 1982

JOYCE HENRIE FUNERAL REMARKS.

In my car I was listening to a tape of "Ashtrays and Gum Wrappers," the talk I'd delivered in 1978 on Mormon and non-Mormon perceptions of living in Utah. I needed to get a quote from it. It jammed. I couldn't untangle it. It had jammed on the section I needed, the section I'd consulted Joyce Henrie about. She'd been a neighbor, a ward friend, a psychiatrist, the only woman on the Salt Lake Clinic staff for twenty-two years, the one doctors and professors and Church authorities chose for their families and themselves, the one loved like few others because she had the gift of making everyone feel important and loved.

Searchers, at that very moment of my tape's jamming, were looking for her across the state, and I didn't know. Missing for a week, her car had been found by snowmobilers in a mountain pass, abandoned, door open. Her husband, John, told me later a psychic in California who'd never been in Utah told the sheriff's office on request exactly where her body was. It was where they had been looking before, even with search dogs. They looked again and found her with avalanche probes on Thanksgiving morning. She'd taken a blanket to lie on and let two feet of snow bury her.

When we heard, we went immediately to visit her husband John. He called me later that night and surprised me by asking if I'd speak at her funeral on Monday. All Friday, Saturday, Sunday, I talked to those who knew her, trying to come to grips with her suicide, trying to find something to say to the hundreds of shocked and mourning patients, family, friends, who needed a blessed kind of comfort.

The talk was still unfinished when I stood at a pulpit in front of those seven hundred who came grieving in a different way from most mourners. They had to be bewildered as I had been four days before. Some of them might be the ten suicide prospects her colleague Dr. Louis Moench had told me might be expected in the wake of Joyce's death up there in the snow. I have come to know her in death in a way I never did in life.

I WONDER HOW many of us on hearing about Joyce's fate last week thought, "There, but for the grace of God, go who knows how many of us?" It was my first thought. It was probably a first thought of anybody who has ever striven for perfection, tried to be everything for everybody, grown weary with well doing. Who of us has not been there?

When I thought of Joyce in the snowy mountains, a Robert Frost poem that I have always loved came to mind.

> *Whose woods these are I think I know.*
> *His house is in the village though.*
> *He will not see me stopping here to watch*
> *The woods fill up with snow. . . .*
>
> *The woods are lovely, dark and deep.*
> *But I have promises to keep*
> *And miles to go before I sleep*
> *And miles to go before I sleep.*

Thinking of the poem brought only more questions. What happens when the puzzle pieces don't fit together? Or when we don't fit? What makes us fit? What makes us think we fit? What makes us think we don't fit and makes us finally drive into the woods instead of away from them?

These are tough questions. For me it was like submerging in some depths that I am not accustomed to, depths that are for me, a nonswimmer, way over my head. I have been engulfed by a kind of despair that finally was dissipated only last night. I am sure I was asking things that many who knew Joyce have asked. Why? Why such waste? Why such despair in someone who had been so able to help the despairing, the disenfranchised, the forsaken, the discouraged, the needy? Also, she has rescued so many who like her were at other times the abundant, the talented, the brilliant, the funny, the humane. She has saved so many others from driving into the snowy woods. Why not herself?

Maybe the mystery of "why" is the saving grace, a mystery never really to be solved but somehow to be understood. I have tried in the last few days to understand by putting the puzzle of Joyce's life together. By making the pieces fit, Joyce put other people's lives together. Surely, I thought, I could understand her death by seeing if I could put her life together. So, I talked to many people and I had many pages of findings. I had a chance to talk with John in the study where Joyce so often saw people. I was able to talk with her family around the kitchen table where she ate. I talked to friends, clients, neighbors, and colleagues, and here is what I was able to piece together.

Picture with me a little girl born the last of ten children. She is given a name that has great significance, Joyce—as in rejoice—and Rich—as in abundance. She is small—small and quick. She loves games, especially Monopoly. As a child, she wins with delight. But she is essentially a private little girl enveloped with ideas that come out of the stacks of books that she brings home from the library to read under the covers at night. When she is seven, she loses her mother. But that mother she refers to constantly, even more than forty years later, in a letter to a daughter, saying: "Dear Lil, My mother left me two legacies—to want to become a doctor and to hold to the values of the Church." In the absence of her mother, she becomes close to her brothers and sisters, now her surrogate parents. When her father remarries, she moves into the relative anonymity of a child in a huge family, although a child far from ordinary, with unique intelligence and rare concerns.

John found tucked away in a drawer the first of many pictures of her in the papers: an eight-year-old who has run into the path of a car to rescue a little dog in danger. There she is holding him safe in her arms. That's what her life was to be—holding something, someone safe in her arms.

She is top in her class wherever she goes, to East High, to South, that mind and heart always at work. She becomes self-supporting. But in a chemistry lab a jar of acid is spilled on her hand, her left hand. It is treated in a hospital with vaseline and wrapping—the worst treatment possible, one that ensures that the burn will go deeper. She loses fingertips and motion that will ironically alter the course of her life. In excruciating pain, she decides that medical care has to be better than this. Interviewing in college for nursing school, she is told: "You cannot be accepted; your hand would be too much of a handicap for you to be a good nurse." Eyeing the woman director calmly, Joyce announces, "Then I will be a doctor."

As a premed student, she is hired as an assistant in a chemistry lab at the University of Utah in 1947. She is instructor of, among others, John Henrie, in his last year of premed. Friends bet John that he cannot get a date with the beautiful but aloof lab instructor. Only weeks before this, Joyce had become friends with John Henrie's mother. Not knowing that her friend had a son on campus, Joyce invited her, "Come see who I am in love with." She took her friend to look in a window where John was studying with three others. "That's my son," said Mrs. Henrie. In their dorm her roommates string a net in the hall to teach her how to hit a ball, how to play with John. They teach her how to dance so she can dance with him. She has rarely taken time to play, too often chastened by the need to work and by urges, says a roommate, to boil bones in the kitchen for anatomy. John and Joyce marry in the Salt Lake Temple in December, 1949, to go through medical school, each with different schedules, but each finagling time to be home in turn with first baby Mary and then second child Lillian.

Twice they are separated for long months, John for a one-year residency at the Mayo Clinic in Minnesota while Joyce finishes her MD at Utah where she is elected Phi Beta Kappa, awarded the AOA status, and graduated top of her class, working as a lab technician and caring for two babies somewhere on the side. She later is also away at the Mayo Clinic for an eighteen-month residency, at the same time studying for her M.S. in psychiatry at the University of Minnesota. There she becomes a student and a close personal friend of Adelaide Johnson, the great child psychologist who dies while Joyce is there—a loss almost like losing her mother again. She has always wanted to study psychiatry. Now she acquires that profession, the profession that will consume her even as it moves and directs her.

Coming home after being a short time in private practice in Arizona, Joyce goes to the Salt Lake Clinic to see Dr. Buzz Sanders about delivering her third baby, Johnny. Some of her classmates in medical school, Allen Barker and DuWayne

Schmidt, are there and remember her exceptional talents. They persuade their colleagues and her that the Clinic must be her professional home.

It becomes that, and for twenty years, (as her close friend, Dr. Louis Moench says) she epitomizes the highest standard of excellence in her personal and professional life. Meticulous in her care of patients, she pursues these standards regardless of cost to herself, refusing to scrimp or take shortcuts. She cares about her patients like her own family. Even when away she makes her phone available to patients or calls them herself from Hawaii or New York. When at Harvard and Massachusetts General, NYU, or Columbia, where she goes to upgrade her expertise, she spends much study time on the phone with patients who need her. On trips her friends and family sometimes wonder at the calls. They don't understand that she gives transfusions of help via the Bell System.

Meantime, at home she is playful with her family. Her children spend much of their time with her on her bed playing spider or Man on the Mountain. She grabs them for a tickle and a hug, always demonstrative, affectionate. She and John are often visiting there in bed, even with little neighbors who come to play and stay, feeling part of the family. She loves chocolate and keeps huge boxes of Cummings' best on her desk for patients and children. She eats chocolate sundaes with Mary for breakfast, drinks chocolate through a straw with Lil while studying, laughs a lot, and drinks Cokes after dinner to stay awake to read after everyone else is long since in bed. She sometimes comes home from San Francisco with a bag of new books bulkier than her suitcase, books for everyone, books for her to find better ways to put together the puzzles of lives that are beginning to take over hers.

Surely she has times like the rest of us when housekeeping and caring for a family are frazzling and demands excruciating as well as replenishing. But the reports from her family never include that. What I hear is whether in work or play, wherever she is, she is thoroughly there, on picnics in Liberty Park, in the sun of Micronesia in a snorkel outfit and a pink bathing suit. She loves the ocean and dipping in to see the life under the surface as much as she loves the wildlife and vegetation of the mountains—and the semi-tamed animals at home. "We always had a pet, Siamese cats one after another," the girls say. "She'd run over one, feel terrible, come home with another as mean as the first, but lovable to her and so to us."

She writes to a daughter away at school, "Study hard and play hard—keep the balance." The chance to keep the balance in her own life gradually erodes as she takes less and less time for play. Her work is so demanding she must program herself to compartmentalize, to be professional and austere with her leisure in order to manage the onslaught of her work. More and more people need her. Even as a hostess she learns to gear herself to the moment, to be totally present in it. She companions John in his wondrous hospitality. Hundreds come to the Henrie home for steaks on the grill, tostados in the kitchen. One Christmas there is an open house for ninety. When Mary, her daughter, not expected home for Christmas from school in Switzerland, shows up at the door just after the dishwasher has broken and the party has run short on food, Joyce greets the late arrival with unflappable cordiality, "Oh, Merry Christmas! Come right in. Would you like something to drink?" and ushers her into the living room. It takes her a full five minutes to register, then she races back to the living room and leaps on Mary's lap laughing, "It's really you!"

She loves to travel with John, play bridge with neighbors—is a wizard at it and would play all night if anyone else would. But patients are asking for still more of her. She becomes the doctor's doctor. "She takes care of more doctors and families, university professors, General Authorities and families than all the rest of us put together," says a colleague. "But," he adds, "she gives the same attention to the humble as to the famous." Some are sensitive and do not want to come to the office so she begins to see them at home. She starts early, ends late. One patient remembers sitting in her office and hearing her tell a caller from New York, "I want very much to talk to you. I want to hear all about what is happening for you, but I am booked solid until midnight. I'll be free to call you by 1:00 A.M. Please just wait. I'll be with you." Everywhere people wait for her, are fed by her for the waiting—and at what personal cost to her? "Of course, it was hard not to have mother all the time, all of her," say the girls. But as Lil notes, "She never missed anything really important to us. And not having her *all* the time made our *some* of the time very precious, a lot to remember."

Eight years after her son Johnny was born, Joyce, now thirty-nine, is sick at Sun Valley. She and John return home early from their vacation. With twinkles in their eyes, they ask their children how they would like to have another member of the family. "Cindy is the family plaything—one we could never have been complete without," says Joyce in an interview.

Joyce's practice becomes fuller, patients recognize her skills and clamor for her time. She is unable to say no. One patient comments, "She has the ability to see the inner person, always the potential. She is honest, believable. She is a safe place." Deeply religious herself, she studies all the great religions in order to better focus that light in the lives of her very diverse clientele. "She is my best friend," say more and more of her patients. There is great reciprocity. Her patients bring much to feed her. But they also learn to depend on her, lean on her.

She becomes a safe place for everyone but herself. She has too much to do, too much to contend with. She is the only woman of now nearly sixty doctors in the Clinic. She crusades to let women know that they are more than appendages. She accepts a reappointment to the admissions committee of the medical school, a big responsibility, a big load, but one she wants to take on. She eats lunch on the run—a sandwich from the receptionist. Dr. Moench notes in retrospect that she was "a doctor of the old school. She cured sometimes, alleviated often, comforted always, made the light glow a little brighter in her own home and kept it alive in countless others." Her colleagues tried to get her to reduce her load, as Dr. Moench remembers, "to about two workhorses worth rather than four."

The holidays are coming—a time very hard on patients. For years she has told her family to plan to celebrate Christmas after New Year's, the demands are so excruciating. She is feeling guilt pains as a mother. There is not enough time, even as she stretches herself thin as gossamer. Over her days, like

Golda Meir, she is thinking always, "Who or what have I neglected today?" Guilt from a sense of inadequacy steals into her ability to put the puzzles together. There have been deaths among those she cares ardently for. She has never just listened. She has always had something positive, tangible to suggest to make the puzzle fit together into a sensible, meaningful whole. She has always been able to deal with the immediate, the now, to dispel griefs of the past.

But now she is weary, discouraged, too much has been drained off. She is planning a sabbatical starting in January to study at Stanford, to begin research—a new, less draining direction—and to be near her daughters and her son, Tom, and grandson, Tommy, whom she adores. It is time to get up from the table where the pieces are spread, to move away from the puzzles of others to put her own together. She has had depres- · sion before. Dr. Moench prescribes medicine that has helped. But too many puzzles remain unsolved. More precious people die, two patients, a sister. She worries about her family, about fragile time, too little time. She has the flu and will not take time to recuperate.

Finally, not even waiting as a professional for the three weeks before the medicine will take effect, she feels completely depleted. What difference can she make? What choice does she have—except to topple? How impossible it often is for any of us to give ourselves permission to be human, vulnerable, weak.

These were the pieces I found and put together after that terrible time of knowing that she was gone. I took the fitted puzzle to sleep with me. There had to be more. Joyce's life could not end in the snowy woods. Too great the contribu-tions. Too distressing the contradictions. By morning I was thinking of the note. Joyce often wrote notes to others when it was too hard to say things. She also wrote notes to herself when her thoughts or feelings were too hard to clarify. There was no suicide note. The last note that she wrote on November 17, a few days before her death, began simply "Our Town. I love that play."

Our Town, Thorton Wilder's remarkable celebration of life. I looked up the play after the night told me to. Some things

Wilder says, Joyce might have carried with her into the woods: "Every child born into the world is nature's attempt to make a perfect human being. We all know that nature is interested in quantity, but I think she is interested in quality too." I found myself saying, You knew it didn't you, Joyce. Maybe because you were unorthodox, you were free to be open to difference, accepting of frailty, not confused by expectation or prejudice and needing no edict but lovingkindness. You were never superficial as a woman, as a homemaker, as a professional. You were thoroughly real and allowed everyone else to be. I know that you have now made peace with so much that conspires to trap us all—doubt, inability, bewilderment at having too much or too little, guilt over not being enough. You knew about human beings and about what Emily says in the play when she dies at twenty-eight: "Oh, I never realized before how troubled and how dark live persons are. From morning until night that's all they are, troubled."

You knew about the trouble, Joyce, and about the aching abundance. When Emily comes back from the eternities to relive her twelfth birthday, she says inaudibly, "Oh, Mama . . . just for a moment now we're all together. Mama, just for a moment we're happy. *Let's look at one another.*" And then, too happy, too nostalgic, she says, "I can't, I can't go on. It goes too fast. We don't have time to look at one another. I didn't realize, so all that was going on and we never noticed. . . . Oh, earth, you're too wonderful for anyone to realize you. Do any human beings ever realize life while they live it—every, every minute?"

Of course Joyce loved *Our Town*—because she realized life every, every minute and allowed other people to do the same. I say to Joyce today: Thank you for bequeathing me not despair. You have delivered me. You have acted out some fate in my stead and you have left me, a virtual stranger, strong and alive and full of hope. Yes, I have promises to keep and miles to go before I sleep. These are my promises to my friend, Joyce Henrie:

> I will take time to look at people that I love.
> I will stay curious about them and my world.

I will not try to take on all of the world's problems
today.
I will take my tired heart to run on the court, around the
block, until frolic and sweat restore me.
I will keep in my life contact with my people one by
one, not let my energies be dissipated in crowds,
lost on triviality.
I will let sleep inform as well as rest me, and never
neglect its power of renewal.
I will be in touch with my God and aware of the touch
of the divine in my promptings every day.
I will find the light in others and nibble away at the
anger in the world.
I will look at the sky and be in favor of trees.
I will cling to the wonder of people and how they fill
me.
I will realize life while I live it, I promise, every, every
minute. With love, Joyce, with love.

I've come alone to my studio this day after the funeral, enriched but also chastened, tired and still unable to dispel the sense of having been taken somewhere I really needed to go but may take a while to come back from.

One by one each of my five daughters, attending the funeral, said to me, "She could be you, Mother. Listen to your promises." It's fantasy to think I could follow all of them any one day. But one or two I can always keep in mind. "Remember Joyce," I will say to myself when ineptitude, folly, and discouragement drag at me. "Remember the promises." They will save me. And make me friends with Time.

*ℬ*ORDERS AND *ℬ*RIDGES

Too often we know each other and our intentions by what we read in the papers or see on television or hear about in isolation from each other.

The gospel of Jesus Christ teaches us that light falls across borders, that the sun in its rotations brightens both sides of a wall, spilling through the spaces in our fences.

APPLAUSE

YESTERDAY THE FIRST SESSION of April general conference ended
with a hymn by the choir, "Where Can I Turn for Peace?" I was
thrilled. It was the second time in just a few weeks that the
Tabernacle Choir had sung that hymn from the new songbook,
a hymn that I wrote the words to and my talented friend,
Joleen Meredith, wrote the music for.

It was more than just another song to me. The text had
come from a time of great sadness and feelings of helplessness
over a daughter's bout with manic depression and bulimia (that
she and I would write a book about twenty years later). It
spoke of my personal struggles and of my urgent petition.

> *Where can I turn for peace?*
> *Where is my solace*
> *When other sources cease to make me whole?*
> *When with a wounded heart,*
> *Anger, or malice,*
> *I draw myself apart,*
> *Searching my soul?*
>
> *Where, when my aching grows,*
> *Where, when I languish,*
> *Where, in my need to know, where can I run?*
> *Where is the quiet hand*
> *To calm my anguish?*
> *Who, who, can understand?*
> *He, only One.*
>
> *He answers privately,*
> *Reaches my reaching,*
> *In my Gethsemane, Savior and Friend.*
> *Gentle the peace he finds*
> *For my beseeching.*
> *Constant he is and kind,*
> *Love without end.*

All of those feelings rushed to remind me again of my struggles when I heard the song yesterday, this time broadcast to nations and continents. It was no different in its message yesterday than it was fifteen years ago talking on the phone from my desk to Joleen at her piano, as she struggled with her own history of genetic depression.

In the same session of conference a Church leader admonished that we not "seek after the applause of the world," because attention to family and church were so much more important in the eyes of the Lord. As I listened to his words and thought of our hymn, I wondered, must applause and attention to "what matters" be mutually exclusive? What more "applause of the world" could an LDS writer hope for than to have one's words heard literally around the globe? Yet who would suggest that the writing of that hymn was with concern for fame or remuneration? I have often been troubled that women, especially, should be asked to shun applause—as if to be successful with one's talents in a "public" way were to desecrate or damage other parts of one's life, particularly spiritual life. I never feel more spiritually attuned than when I write or more spiritually bereft than when I don't.

How different was writing that hymn from my writing whatever else I write? To the artist, all expression is imperative—if it is honest. And if the imperative is there, no denial of it can make for happiness, either for the artist or for those who live close to her or him.

A few years before his death, the remarkable writer Truman Capote read at the University of Utah. After completely captivating a packed crowd with his much acclaimed story "A Christmas Memory," he invited questions. "Why did you write that story?" a bulky young law student asked, obviously moved. Capote, small enough that his gnomelike head barely showed above the podium, paused for what seemed like an eon, thinking, the audience hushed. Then in his childlike lisp he answered, "Because I had to."

I've never forgotten that. Of course, that's why Willa Cather or Emily Dickinson or Eliza R. Snow wrote what they did. Not, I think, with potential applause ringing in their ears. Of course, they wanted to be read, as did Capote, egoist supreme. But to condemn a writer because something succeeds, or for the impetus to write for someone else to see, is to deny genes and instinct, to let lights go out under bushels before they even make it to the hill.

Not long ago I was on a program with two winners of the state's most prestigious writing awards: a woman who won first place for her nature column in the *Deseret News* from the Utah Society of Professional Journalists, and another who won the BYU Award for Excellence for a biography.

Each of us took some time to talk about what we wrote, how, and why. We could not have been more different in what and how, nor more alike in why. The one, Terry Tempest Williams, is a thirty-year-old curator of a natural history museum, young wife, lover of the outdoors, whose studies have acquainted her with every feather and stone under any intriguing sky. She writes poetic books for children. The other, Linda King Newell, is a mother of teenagers, a historian whose research had taken eight years to compile into a straightforward account of events over which she had no control except to present them clearly and objectively for an adult readership. I was a writer of poetry, fiction, and essays, a lover of words, and a teacher of literature. Each of us was writing because she had to. Earning royalties would be happy serendipity. Any applause there might be came way down the line. This I know because I know those women.

And I know me. I write because nothing seems really to have happened to me until I write about it—a new baby, a trip to Russia, a doubt or a joy—clarification and catharsis by writing are built into my system as surely as faith in "my Savior and Friend."

Maybe what I keep hoping for women is that we will be nurtured and encouraged in our talents as Brigham Young encouraged women in his day—to spend ourselves on what only we can do, to write the book, paint the painting, compose the music, dance the dance, decorate the cake, edit the paper, crochet the afghan, design the house, paper the dining room, whatever our impulses and talents carry us toward—that we receive encouragement with cooperation from our families, just as it's given to men to spur them to the applause of the world if they deserve it. My experience has shown that just as no success may compensate for failure in the home, so no success in the home can compensate for failure to be all that one can be anywhere else. So many women whom I love and respect have demonstrated success in both to the detriment of neither. It takes Herculean effort, and any applause that they might receive in either place can never be too much.

Because God gave the talent, and with it came the equally God-given urgency to *have* to.

BORDER CROSSINGS

IT HAPPENED AGAIN AS I was walking through the New Hampshire woods with a woman I knew only slightly. We had been chatting amiably when the words "Mormon feminist" escaped my mouth. From the expression on her face, I knew exactly what she was going to say.

"Mormon feminist! That sounds like an oxymoron!"

I bristled, though I didn't mean to, annoyed at having to explain myself once again.

Yes, I am an active, believing Mormon. I was baptized at the age of eight, graduated from seminary, and married in the Salt Lake Temple. For thirty-five years I have tried to remain true to my temple covenants, including the one about consecrating time and talents to the Church. I have taught early morning seminary, written road shows, edited the stake newsletter, and picked apples, plums, peaches, and pears at the stake welfare farm. With my husband, I recently completed my third stint as Gospel Doctrine teacher in our ward.

And, yes, in the tradition of my Mormon heritage, I am a feminist. I deplore teachings, policies, or attitudes that deny women their full stature as human beings, and I have tried to act on that conviction in my personal and professional life. I have written two books and more than a dozen articles on women's history. I give money to the day care coalition in my town and the women's political caucus in my state. I helped draft my university's non-sexist language policy.

I am quite aware that some people consider those commitments incompatible. A couple of years ago, a member of the Women's Commission at my university, learning that I was a Mormon, said in astonishment, "I am surprised your church hasn't thrown you out long ago."

"Thrown me out!" I gasped. "I'm a pillar of my congregation." The very same day I was queried by an LDS acquaintance I had not seen for several years. Hearing about my awards for feminist scholarship, she asked earnestly, "Do you go to church? Do you bear your testimony?" I groaned and told her, tongue in cheek, I was an "agnostic Gospel Doctrine teacher."

Perhaps my disposition to stand apart is genetic. Elsewhere I have written about my Thatcher progenitors, stalwart pioneers who regularly disagreed with church authorities. I have said less about my maternal ancestors, the Siddoways. In my mother's hometown, I am told, there are still three ways of doing things—the right way, the wrong way, and the Siddoway. Graduate school compounded what family inheritance and eight years of high school and college debate began. I am afraid I fit the definition of an intellectual as "a person who thinks otherwise." Hence when I began this essay more than a year ago, I entitled it "Confessions of an OxyMormon." According to my dictionary, the prefix *oxy* means "sharp, keen, acute, pungent, acid," not a bad description for one given to critical thinking. I admit to preferring vinegar to honey, being less interested in catching flies than in rousing the faint.

Yet I am not so sure I want to admit to *all* the implications of the epithet. Acid can burn as well as cleanse, and in my dictionary, the word "keen" slides along an enticing but slippery lexical path from "wise, learned, clever, and brave" to "proud, forward, and insolent." Against such dangers my Mormonism buzzes: "O the vainness, and the frailties, and the foolishness of men! When they are learned they think they are wise, and they hearken not unto the counsel of God" (2 Ne. 9:28). As an intellectual I am forced to question my questioning. As a Latter-day Saint I acknowledge my foolishness (and precociously gender specific); the meaning is unmistakable.

Last winter the *Boston Globe* ran a story on *Exponent II* under the headline "Challenging the Mormon Church." The author, freelance writer Suzanne Gordon, had worked hard on her essay, interviewing members and nonmembers, scholars and activists, and attending at least one meeting of the newspaper staff. "To an outsider," she confessed, "the very act of understanding these women requires a minicourse in cross-cultural studies." Building on interviews with two non-LDS historians, she concluded that the editors and writers of *Exponent II* were not only risking censure in this world but salvation in the after-life. In the context of Mormon theology, she concluded, "any talk about a female identity outside of the family, or critical consideration of the problems of family life, can be taken as a fundamental challenge to the very foundation of Mormonism itself."[1] My youngest son, a man of quiet good sense who lives in a converted warehouse in the heart of bohemian Boston, said that while he enjoyed the article, he thought the author "exaggerated the rebellion." He was amused that the sturdy Mormon Mother he knew, a habitual reader of scriptures and monitor of hair length, could ever be seen as "shaking the foundations of the Church."[2]

He is right. I am not an oxyMormon. I am a Mormon. And a feminist. As a daughter of God, I claim the right to all my gifts. I am a mother, an intellectual, a skeptic, a believer, a crafter of cookies and words. I am not a Jack (or a Jill) in a Box, ready to jump when my button is pushed.

Perhaps I am comfortable wearing the feminist label because as a Latter-day Saint living in the East I have had so much practice being an oddball. Shortly after we moved to Massachusetts in 1960, I succumbed to the entreaties of the missionaries in our ward and agreed to help with a telephone survey. We were to ask each person on our list the Golden Questions: What do you know about the Mormon church? Would you like to know more? One man silenced me by responding, "I don't know a thing about the Mormon Church, but I shall look it up in my *Encyclopedia Britannica* immediately." His smug tolerance put me in my place—in the M's, somewhere between Moonbeam and Moron.

I doubt his encyclopedia had an entry for "feminism." Although the word was in common use in the United States between 1895 and 1930, it fell out of fashion before World War II, not to be revived again until the 1970s. My *Compact Oxford English Dictionary*, copyright 1971, defines feminism as "the qualities of females." Until 1977, the index to *The Reader's Guide to Periodical Literature* cross-referenced the word under "Woman—social and moral questions." It is really rather startling to think that in July 1974, a group of Massachusetts housewives could launch a quarterly newspaper, *Exponent II*, "on the dual platforms of Mormonism and Feminism." We did not think we had committed an oxymoron.

Today, the computerized catalog at the University of New Hampshire library lists 777 books under the subject entry "Feminism." Obviously, any movement as large, as fast growing, and as complex as this one cannot be reduced to a simple definition. When I hear people rail against feminists, I always wonder who they mean. Scholars have differentiated among radical feminism, liberal feminism, Marxist feminism, Christian feminism, lesbian feminism, and more. Pushing the concept back in time, they have coined terms like *domestic feminism, social feminism, material feminism, relational feminism,* and *proto-feminism.*[3] Long before there was an organized women's rights movement, there were women who struggled against arbitrary limits on their humanity. Though my dictionary doesn't have a definition for feminism as we know it, it does have an entry for *bluestocking,* a term coined about 1750 and applied "sneeringly to any woman showing a taste for learning."

When I say that I am a feminist, I identify with women across the centuries who have had the courage to claim their own gifts. Theologically, I don't have much in common with the Puritan poet Anne Bradstreet, but having been raised in a culture that simultaneously nurtures and mistrusts female achievement, I can identify with her words:

> *I am obnoxious to each carping tongue*
> *Who says my hand a needle better fits. . .*
> *For such despite they cast on female wits;*
> *If what I do prove well, it won't advance,*
> *They'll say it's stolen, or else it was by chance.*[4]

There was no organized women's rights movement in seventeenth-century Massachusetts, but there was something like feminism.

As a Mormon, I embrace ideals of equality and a critique of power that also shaped early feminism. Abigail Adams' statement "all Men would be tyrants if they could"[5] is not far removed from Joseph Smith's "We have learned by sad experience that it is the nature and disposition of almost all men as soon as they get a little authority, as they suppose, they will immediately begin to exercise unrighteous dominion" (D&C 121:39). Mormonism rejects the Calvinist notion of predestination as well as the monarchical notion of a great chain of being in which each person is subordinate to the one above. Listen to Lehi: "And because that they are redeemed from the fall they have become free forever, knowing good from evil; to act for themselves and not to be acted upon" (2 Ne. 2:26). Lehi's formulation is surprisingly close to the modern distinction between subject and object. That each person be free to think, speak, and act for herself is both a feminist and a Mormon dream. As a Latter-day Saint, I say with Mary Wollstonecraft, "Let not men then in the pride of power, use the same arguments that tyrannic kings and venal ministers have used and fallaciously assert that woman ought to be subjected because she has always been so."[6]

Yet my commitment to the church of Jesus Christ pushes me beyond a mere concern for "rights." As a feminist I know that structures matter, that formal authority makes a difference in the way people think as well as behave, that institutional arrangements can lock in prejudice, yet I also know that legal protection is hollow without spiritual transformation and that the right spirit can transform a seemingly repressive system. My daily experience as a Latter-day Saint confirms the words of Margaret Fuller, a nineteenth-century feminist and contemporary of Joseph Smith: "Were thought and feeling once so far elevated that Man should esteem himself the brother and friend, but nowise the lord and tutor, of Woman—were he really bound with her in equal worship—arrangements as to function and employment would be of no consequence."[7] I have tasted equal worship in The Church of Jesus Christ of Latter-day Saints. Unfortunately, I have also observed the smug condescension of men who believe they have been called as lord and tutor. Against such behavior I assert both my Mormonism and my feminism.

To claim multiple identities is to assert the insufficiency of any one label, including Mormonism. According to my compact *Oxford English Dictionary*, an oxymoron is not simply a self-contradictory expression like *freezing heat* or *swampy desert*. It is a rhetorical figure in which contradictory or incongruous terms are intentionally joined in order to complicate or enlarge meaning. Although in current usage the word is "often loosely or erroneously used as if merely a contradiction in terms," a true oxymoron is "an expression in its superficial or literal meaning self-contradictory or absurd, but involving a point." The phrase "Mormon feminist" can work that way. Those who assume that Mormonism is inherently hostile to women or, conversely, that feminism undermines faith, sniff at the phrase. But when confronted with a real person claiming to be both things at once, they are forced to reconsider their assumptions. Feminism may be larger than they imagined and Mormonism more flexible.

As biologist Stephen Jay Gould has written, "We must categorize and simplify in order to comprehend. But the reduction of complexity entails a great danger, since the line between enlightening epitome and vulgarized distortion is so fine."[8] *The Boston Globe* crossed that line when it described The Church of Jesus Christ of Latter-day Saints as "quintessentially misogynist."[9] But when anxious Church leaders denounce feminists they compound the distortion. Each group reduces the other to its own worst nightmare, and the war is on. In such a climate it is tempting to run for shelter, saying less about feminism among Mormons and less about Mormonism everywhere else. But a silence based on fear is no solution. As long as the issues are there, unacknowledged and unresolved, the anger and hostility will remain. I think it is better to gently but consistently tell the truth. I am a Mormon and a feminist.

I remember as a teenager standing up in my ward in Sugar City, Idaho, to repeat the MIA theme of the year: "Let no man despise thy youth; but be thou an example of the believers, in word, in conversation, in charity, in spirit, in faith, in purity" (1 Tim. 4:12). I am grateful for a religious education that taught me how to be different, though I had no idea it would sometimes make me feel like a stranger among the Saints. In my generation, being an example of the believers had a lot to do with the Word of Wisdom. In Sunday School and MIA, we learned about the Mormon lad who resisted a proffered cup of coffee or a drink only to be rewarded with a promotion. (Nobody told us the promotion might be the biggest danger of all!) Fortunately, in the old seminary room above the Sugar City Theatre, a mandolin-playing teacher named Ken Brown taught a more complex ethic. Gently and with humor, he led us through the New Testament, helping us to see the dangers in the Pharisees' attempt to separate themselves from the ungodly. The harder they tried to behave as "Abraham's children," the less they were capable of receiving the Messiah when he came.

A few years ago I attended an invitational conference in U.S. women's history. The organizers, fully committed to diversity, had gone out of their way to include women from large and small colleges, from every part of the United States, and from many minority groups. When one scholar expressed surprise that no one from BYU had been invited, a well-known nineteenth-century historian responded, "Oh, we don't want *them!*" Orthodoxy feels the same wherever it is found. Certainly there is a need for boundaries, for rigorous defense of ideas and ideals that matter, but defenders of every faith too often violate their own ideals in the very act of defending them. The gospel of Jesus Christ teaches us that light falls across borders, that the sun in its revolutions brightens both sides of a wall, spilling through the spaces in our fences. Mormon intellectuals should not forget that Jesus gathered his disciples from among sinners, publicans, *and* Pharisees, even zealous Pharisees like Paul, a man who knew what it meant to live in a multicultural world. To the Saints at Ephesus, Paul wrote: "For he is our peace, who hath made both one, and hath broken down the middle wall of partition between us" (Eph. 2:14).

Recently I assigned Tzvetan Todorov's *The Conquest of America* to my students in early American history. While reading it again, I found personal meaning in the closing section which relates the story of the Spanish conquest to the problems of pluralism in our own times. In Todorov's view, one of the few Spaniards who was able to transcend the brutality and condescension that characterized early Spanish treatment of the Indians was Cabeza de Vaca, an explorer who spent eight years lost in the interior of North America. It wasn't only that Cabeza had experienced both cultures from within, it was that after his exile he never fully belonged to either. Without becoming an Indian, he "was no longer quite a Spaniard." For Todorov, Cabeza illuminates the mysterious words of Hugh of St. Victor: "The man who finds his country sweet is only a raw beginner; the man for whom each country is as his own is already strong; but only the man for whom the whole world is as a foreign country is perfect." Todorov's insight helped me to reassess the dislocations in my own life. I have sometimes felt like a woman without a country. Perhaps that experience of "otherness" can be a source of strength. We are all prisoners of culture, bound not by visible laws but by a net of assumptions and prejudices we cannot see. In the space between competing identities, I seek Lehi's freedom.

I do not apologize for what I am—an intellectual who reveres the scriptures; a Sunbeam teacher who would sooner write than eat; a transplanted Westerner at home in the East. I can no more deny my religious identity than I can divest myself of my Thatcher freckles or my Rocky Mountain accent. Nor would I discard my feminist values. The women's movement has refreshed my life like the "sea change" that sometimes hits my town on those steamy, grey days so common on the east coast in midsummer. At such moments a blue, almost western, sky breaks through the haze.

Notes

1 Suzanne Gordon, *Boston Globe*, March 25, 1993, reprinted in *Exponent II*, 17:4, 5–7.

2 *Ibid*, 6.

3 For a useful discussion of the historical origins of the term *feminism*, see Nancy F. Cott, "What's in a Name? The Limits of 'Social Feminism': or, Expanding the Vocabulary of Women's History," *Journal of American History* 76 (1989): 809–29. Although I agree with Cott's plea for an expanded vocabulary for female activism, I can think of no substitute

for "feminism" when used in a broader context.

[4] Anne Bradstreet, "The Prologue," *The Norton Anthology of Literature by Women*, ed. Sandra M. Gilbert and Susan Gubar (New York: W.W. Norton, 1985), 62

[5] Abigail Adams to John Adams, March 31, 1776, in *The Feminist Papers*, ed. Alice S. Rossi (New York: Bantam Books, 1973), 10.

[6] From *A Vindication of the Rights of Woman* (1790), excerpted in *Feminist Papers*, 58.

[7] *Feminist Papers*, 164.

[8] "Triumph of a Naturalist," *New York Review of Books*, March 19, 1984: 58–71, quoted in Cynthia Fuchs Epstien, *Deceptive Distinctions: Sex, Gender, and the Social Order* (New Haven and London: Yale University Press, 1988), frontispiece.

[9] Suzanne Gordon, "Herstory in the Making," *Boston Globe Magazine*, January 31, 1993, reprinted in *Exponent II*, 17:4, 4.

YOU TELL ME YOUR DREAMS
AND I'LL TELL YOU MINE

Cookies in the Airport

Cookies. Pepperidge Farm Milanos. Just a few. Perfect for between flights. Buy a bag to put down with your belongings on the seat between you and the man also waiting down the row. Pick up your mystery novel, get absorbed, pass the forty-five minute layover with no anxieties.

Fine. But then . . . what? That man. What's he doing? Reaching for your bag of cookies? Opening it? Taking a cookie out! Surely not. You look his way, try to be nonchalant, wonder what in the world . . . ?

So you reach into the bag, take one of your own, looking intently at your book. Let him know just whose bag of cookies that is. But then . . . surely not again. He's taking another cookie. Two! Eating them as if he'd done nothing wrong. The nerve, the very nerve. And he looks like such a nice man, smiling the whole time, not at you, but at the newspaper he's *reading. Or pretending to. Like you with your book, now far from your focus but a great prop.*

He reaches for the bag, takes two more cookies. You do the same, neither looking at the other but seeing it all. Again him. Again you. Finally, the end. He reaches in, rustles his hand around in the bottom of the bag, and takes the last cookie! Oh come on! Do you accuse him? Give him a vampire look? Tip the empty bag over in his face? Make him somehow aware? At least let him know that you know?

He's standing up now, picking up his carry-on, and smiling. Smiling right at you, nodding as if he were the most pleasant man in the airport. Really? Not a word, not an apology?

You stand to gather your coat, your purse, your own carry-on. You fumble for your ticket as you head for the line-up to the flight. He's now gone off to another gate. May his destination be jail!

You keep fumbling, watching him go. Then . . . oh, come on. Not really. In your purse, a bag of cookies.

THIS STORY HAS to be an urban legend. Nearly six months after I'd written the story that I'd heard from a friend who had heard it in church, another version surfaced at a gathering in New Hampshire. This time the source was British, the cookies, tea biscuits, and the setting a pub. Regardless of setting, what little bit of talk could have cleared up whose cookies were being eaten? How much just plain interest instead of indignation—or for him amusement—could have suggested a simple question, to reach across the chasm of misunderstanding? Might that exchange, any exchange, have turned the encounter into something worthwhile? Instead, two people went their ways impoverished for being too proud or shy or maybe too indifferent to find the truth.

Meantime, in the real world of our relating to each other as women, as friends or strangers, or as members and leaders in or out of Church settings, misunderstandings can arise from lack of letting each other in on who and where we are. This can be especially true in our impressions of our General Authorities. Too often we draw those impressions from what we read in the papers or see on television or hear about in isolation from each other. The media's attempts at objective reporting often end up slanted one way or another. What "hearings" we have among any of us, especially among women, are too often via preconceived assumptions, as with the cookies, focused on who lays claim to what. Can such assuming bring about anything but divisiveness? Instead of talking, we become victims of our own distancing.

But bridging the distances can be difficult even among those who care about the same causes and people. About a year ago, I had an experience that made me think about this, particularly in relation to what we know about our Church leaders.

Our monthly meeting of the *Deseret News* board of directors always started at three sharp in a room where another meeting was going overtime. In that room at 47 East South Temple where the First Presidency and the Twelve meet, we of the board also had our regular meetings with President Thomas Monson and Elder James Faust presiding. Other members of the board were Bishop Victor Brown, Elder Neal Maxwell, BYU president Dallin Oaks and later Jeffrey Holland, advertising executive and former newsman Glen Snarr, bank president Bob Bischoff, and me.

For sixteen years I'd dangled or slumped in order to occupy the too-large leather armchair next to the publisher and across from the editor of the paper and Bob Bischoff. He and I had kidded about being "token" on the board, he the one nonmember, I the lone woman. Those had been eventful years of budgets and bottom lines, advertising and circulation reports, attention to editorial and page makeup, news holes, news, and the price of newsprint. We had toured newsrooms and presses, watched writers move from the clatter of rooms full of typewriters to the muted ticking of computers as stories and artwork appeared on screens to be paginated, printed, and tossed on porches like fields of energy with information packaged for perusal.

I had loved and respected the whole process. And the people who made it happen.

Yes, and also those men in the chairs surrounding the table under the paintings of Joseph Smith and President Benson. I was surprised to calculate that in those nearly seventeen years we'd had more than two hundred meetings together in that room, plus as many other meetings in offices in that building or at the paper, plus dinners and lunches with and without spouses, Christmas cards and parties, summer cookouts and the weddings and funerals of each others' loved ones. We'd shared pulpits and publishings, jokes and concerns. We were friends. And we were engaged in a common cause.

Now, those of us not General Authorities waited on the huge blue Oriental rug under the lights of brass and mother-of-pearl sconces of the inner entry as those who daily occupied that pillared building finished their business inside. When the great brown door opened, we of the board inadvertently formed a line to go in. Out streamed two of the Church presidency, all the apostles, the heads of Relief Society, Young Women, and Primary, and the president of BYU, cordial as at a wedding, shaking hands as they passed, only a few with the grab-and-move-along-as-fast-as-possible handshake acquired in too many confrontations with thronging. I knew well all but the newest apostle, Elder Richard G. Scott. I'd been school-mates with many; my husband, with others.

That night I thought, and have since, what good men and women are called to give their all to run this great leviathan of a church. How I would hate to have their jobs, especially being subject to a kind of scrutiny that would beleaguer a microbe under a microscope. I felt the burden of their callings and the potential for misunderstanding between their deliberations and even the doings of the next meeting in the room they had just left—let alone between them and the multitudes who see them only on television or in the *Church News*, the millions whose stories they can never be privy to in the making of their world-wide decisions any more than those millions can know those decisionmakers and the backgrounds and personalities that have shaped them. How can the hundreds, thousands, now millions like me interpret and internalize every word and move in terms of our own unique findings and flounderings, securi-ties and struggles, all of it as personal as the connection by media is distant?

Add to this the bludgeoning of opinion, misinformation, out-of-context assumptions, time pressures, overcommitment for most of us and certainly for them—and how do we expect to hear, let alone understand, each other's stories? Yet it is that hearing that can make all the difference. When we hear each other, and more importantly understand, we recognize that we are all trying our level best to paddle well and stay afloat in our seas of dailiness and demands and wanting to do better.

I grew up in a church as personal and approachable as that lineup outside the door in the Church Administration Building. I believe still in the private exchange. I believe, too, that we need each other, those on either end of a handshake and gen-uine, "How are you?"

In his 1994 Christmas address, newly sustained president and prophet Howard W. Hunter translates the Beatitudes of Jesus into concrete, present-tense application. From an editorial in a women's publication, *McCall's* magazine, he draws some

directives to frame a message. Even a few of his simple imperative sentences make an impressive list:

This Christmas,
  Mend a quarrel.
  Dismiss suspicion and replace it with trust.
  Write a letter.
  Give a soft answer.
  Forgo a grudge.
  Try to understand.
  Examine your demands on others.
  Think first of someone else.
  Be kind.
  Laugh a little more.
  Welcome a stranger.
  Take pleasure in the beauty and wonder of the world.
  Speak your love and then speak it again.

To these he adds his own motive of the soul, "All with the
sudden stirring of the heart that has extended itself unselfishly
in the things that matter most."

A long list? Maybe. But love swells in President Hunter's
every imperative. What might acting on any one of these essentials, for even an hour, do to turn a stiff or wilting or charged
relationship into a profoundly changed one? Acting on such
counsel, how could divisiveness occur among us women or
between us and the authorities we encounter? So why the label-
ing? Why the "us" and the "them," the suspicion of each other's
motives, the defining other's as being in or out of the gospel
mainstream by judgments, and surface evaluations?

Can we be delivered from our history of persecution, or are
we doomed to repeat it in our persecution of each other?
Instead, can we listen to and follow President Hunter's simple
directions?

Nothing really counts so much as how we regard and treat
each other. If the Church in Joseph Smith's time and in my
growing up years drew together people of varying backgrounds and groundings, can it not be so for women now?
When will we be able to let go of labels and recognize that we

do need each other? We need not agree with everyone's point of view, but we need to respect each person's right to differ. We need to hear each other's stories and to understand, not fear or ostracize or condemn each other at the various stages of our questing as well as following.

Application of the basic admonitions of President Hunter's references could draw us into places of peace in our dealings with even someone we regard as an "enemy." Imagine the effect of applying "Give a soft answer" or "Forgo a grudge" or "Welcome a stranger" in the Cookies story. Especially imagine "Think first of someone else" or "Laugh a little more." What kind of good time might the two with hands in the bag of cookies have had laughing at the misunderstanding?

More privately, in our relationship with the Lord, imagine waking up on any morning thinking, "Take pleasure in the beauty and wonder of the world." President Hunter pulls principles into view and converts them to human possibility, all in a context of asking, "What would Jesus do?"

In somewhat the same way, C. S. Lewis says, "I believe in Jesus Christ as I do in the rising sun—not that I can see it, but by it, I see everything else more clearly." President Hunter offers glasses for the rest of us to see differently by doing differently.

No, those authorities whose hands I shook and warmth I felt coming out of their meeting that day cannot always respond personally. But in following Christ, anyone—leaders or otherwise—from General Authorities to bishops to visiting teachers to neighbors across the street to friends in the foyer can offer solace through listening to honest concerns and responding. In that comforting exchange we send love to each other. In our prayers we do the same. We must not push away at the very time when we need each other most. We must listen and talk and try to understand rather than judge and label.

More than anything, we must trust each other. Trust that our dreams can be told and that they will, in the big picture, be surprisingly alike. In two recent conferences of LDS women from the East and Midwest, I felt, instead of a sense of oppression, a sense of hope—hope for the power of prayer and the reality of answers to it. One woman, Jolene Robison, who died

211

only months later, suggested that we circle on our calendars the last day of every month and set it aside for special prayers for women in Somalia, men in the UN armed forces, children in the streets, babies born and unborn, and for those in authority in our LDS faith to feel the sincerity of our wanting to shake their hands and wish them well and offer the very best we have to the causes and dreams we share. This we can do, through the divine connections we know are as real as any handshake in any coming together anywhere.

Meanwhile, when the storms crash about me, I know that the ultimate turning for peace is inward. Like a lightning rod in a thunderstorm, I can stay grounded in the peaceable and let the storms lend, instead of fear, the power through which I operate. We can trust in the love of Christ to supply the grounding, even as we return light for light, like sparklers in the dark, saying, You are, I am, and we are eligible for any reaching our reaching might persuade—in any one of the Beatitudes illuminated by a gentle, wise, modern-day prophet of the Lord.

Bless us all to "speak our love then speak it again," no matter what rooms we occupy or dreams we dare to dream. After all, it was Joseph Smith's daring to ask, to dream, and then to remain in touch with both the human and the divine that started our meeting together in the first place.

Note
¹This essay has been adapted from a presentation at the 1993 BYU Women's Conference on the theme "Women in the Covenant of Grace." The Original text appears in the volume of selected talks from this conference, published by Deseret Book Co., 1994.

SNORE

MY HUSBAND IS STARTING a new society. One of our children suggested he call it the Spiritual Nodders Organization for Restoring Energy—acronym SNORE. But he has settled on the less imaginative, but more accurate title, SICA, Sleepers In Church Anonymous. The prospectus of his new organization explains that sleeping in church is an illness that can best be controlled through mutual help and support. Gael hopes that those afflicted will begin to band together for discussion (and hot fudge brownies) after church.

I am sure that one of the first topics for discussion will be the judgmental attitudes of other people. The prospectus admits that church sleeping "appears to afflict brethren more than sisters and seldom strikes both partners in a marriage," then goes on to lament that "among those who are never hit, the malady is least understood, explaining perhaps their intolerance and abuse of those who are suffering."

Gael is quite right. He is an accomplished sleeper. I am an accomplished abuser. I poke him when he is not sitting on the stand. When he is, I focus the full power of my gaze upon him, hoping that the intensity of my dismay will reach him somewhere in the blissful fog to which he has escaped. It seldom does, but you can be sure I let him know when we get home that his holding an open notebook didn't fool anyone. How can anyone go to sleep in front of a hundred and fifty people? Perhaps it was destined from the beginning. After all, the book of Genesis tells us that God "caused a deep sleep to fall upon Adam" (Gen. 2:21).

In New England three hundred years ago, awakening sleepers was a recognized church calling. In one congregation, a man named Allen Bridges was assigned to walk around the meetinghouse during the sermon carrying a long staff. On one end of his pole was a fox tail for arousing nappers, on the other a sharp thorn to "prick such as be most sound." The fox tail failed to arouse a certain Brother Tomling one warm June day, so Bridges gave him an energetic prick on his hand with results that startled the entire congregation. One man recorded the incident this way in his diary:

Mr. Tomling did spring up much above the floor, and with terrible force strike his hand against the wall; and also, to the great wonder of all, profanely exclaimed in a loud voice, "Curse the woodchuck," he dreaming so it seemed that a woodchuck had seized and bit his hand. But on coming to know where he was, and the great scandal he had committed, he seemed much abashed, but did not speak. And I think he will not soon again goe to sleep in meeting.[1]

Among the Puritans, institutional pressure and public humiliation kept sleeping within bounds, even if it didn't eliminate it entirely. In some Latter-day Saint wards, the block meeting schedule has greatly reduced sleeping, it being easier to pay attention at nine A.M. than at five P.M. But some people I will not name can sleep through a sermon at any time of day or night. Surely there must be more we can do to help them.

The scriptures indicate that somnolence in meetings is an ancient phenomenon—especially in hot weather. The book of Acts records the story of a young man named Eutychus who was sitting in an open window during one of Paul's sermons in Troas. The sermon had gone on until midnight. The night was probably warm and the lamps hot, and whatever air came through the windows was insufficient to keep Eutychus awake. He "sunk down with sleep" and fell out the window "from the third loft." The worried Christians took him up for dead, but Paul was not dismayed. With compassion he raised the injured man and blessed him, then went back inside, broke bread, and preached the rest of the night (Acts 20:9–12). As far as I can tell, no one had anything but compassion for Eutychus.

I hope Gael's society is just as successful in bringing aid and comfort to Latter-day nodders. In my experience, men who sleep in church are almost always good men, some of the best, the sort who show up for service projects, pay tithes and offerings willingly, and stay up until three in the morning working on ward finances or a child's new bed. They don't deserve our condemnation—just a gentle tickle to the chin or a prick on the side. I suggest we match them up with the wiggliest children in the ward. That would solve two problems, and no one would have to be embarrassed.

Note
[1] Alice Morse Earle, *The Sabbath in Puritan New England,* 1891.

RESIST NOT EVIL

THE DOCTRINE & COVENANTS TELLS us that "it is the nature and disposition of almost all men, as soon as they get a little authority, as they suppose, they will immediately begin to exercise unrighteous dominion" (D&C 121:39). In the larger context of Joseph Smith's teachings, this passage is astonishingly pessimistic. The Prophet didn't say *some* men or *quite a few* but *almost all*. Nor did he allow much latitude for the burdens of leadership that sometimes provoke kind men to behave in autocratic ways. He said that in many people the impulse to control and dominate others is *immediate*, that it is a direct and almost overwhelming consequence of getting "a little authority, as they suppose."

My own experience with authority, particularly with Church authority, has been more positive. Most of the Church leaders I have known have been genuinely loving if not always wise. Last winter, however, I had an experience almost anyone would have called "unrighteous dominion." I was both angry and sad, outraged at what appeared to me to be a flagrant abuse of Church authority, dismayed at my own inability to do anything about it. One morning I awoke with a scripture—or at least what I thought was a scripture—planted firmly in my head. *Resist not evil; hold fast to that which is good.* I slipped out of bed, tiptoed through the still dark house to find my standard works and an extra blanket, then curled onto an empty bed under the east window in our guest room. As the morning light penetrated the room, I found the words I was looking for. Not one verse but two, mysteriously joined, "resist not evil" from Matthew and "hold fast that which is good" from 1 Thessalonians.

I felt mild disappointment when I discovered that the first half of my couplet came from a passage in the Sermon on the Mount I find troublesome: "I say unto you, That ye resist not evil: but whosoever shall smite thee on thy right cheek, turn to him the other also" (Matt. 5:39). The problem with that advice, I thought, is not that it is too difficult, but that it is too easy, particularly in situations where there is gross disparity in authority or power. I thought of the nineteenth-century South, a place filled with Bible-reading masters who happily paid ministers to teach Christian meekness to their slaves. I thought, too, of all I had learned in recent years about family violence. Brute power feeds on learned helplessness. Telling an abused person to turn the other cheek may reinforce her feelings of inferiority, adding strength to an already well-developed belief that the other person's behavior is her responsibility. If she were better—more loving, more gentle, more sophisticated, more anything else you can think of—this wouldn't be happening. I didn't want to fall into that trap in my own relationship with authority.

Later I was relieved to find a similar concern in James E. Talmage's *Jesus the Christ.* Talmage insists that the admonition to turn the other cheek should "not be construed as commanding abject subservience to unjust demands, nor as an abrogation of the principle of self-protection." Unfortunately, he didn't say much about the practical problem of distinguishing just from unjust demands. He further complicated his interpretation by suggesting that Christ's command to turn the other cheek was "directed primarily to the apostles." Because their mission was to build the kingdom, "it would be better to suffer material loss or personal indignity and imposition at the hands of wicked oppressors, than to bring about an impairment of efficiency and hindrance in work through resistance and contention."[1]

Did he mean that ordinary Church members could stand up for themselves whenever necessary but that priesthood leaders should accept whatever abuse the world offered? I don't believe that was his point. I think he was saying that the ability to turn the other cheek grows as we accept the responsibilities of Christian discipleship. The point was not to ignore injustice but to avoid being distracted by it. I thought about the way my own feelings of anger and betrayal had gotten in the way of my work during the previous week. I had been so concerned about injustices perpetrated against me, I had forgotten the things I really wanted to do and was fully capable of doing. *Resist not evil.* Good advice, I thought, for members as well as Church leaders. The idea seemed even more powerful when combined with the other half of the couplet, the verse from 1 Thessalonians 5:21: "*. . . hold fast that which is good.*" For me the meaning was unmistakable. The true Christian doesn't hit back, but neither does she sit passively waiting for the next blow. She overcomes evil by persisting in doing good.

That isn't easy. The most frightening thing about an abusive relationship is the way it gets inside, magnifying self-doubts, cankering the spirit. It takes genuine courage to choose a course of action and stick with it when your own worst enemy has taken up residence in your psyche.

How can we know the good? Paul gives his answer in four crisp verses,

> "*Pray without ceasing.*" (*verse 17*)
> "*Quench not the Spirit.*" (*verse 19*)
> "*Despise not prophesyings.*" (*verse 20*)
> "*Prove all things; hold fast that which is good.*" (*verse 21*)

Paul doesn't say, "If in doubt, ask your bishop" (though I wouldn't mind asking mine). He says, "Work at discovering the good." He invites us to learn both through direct inspiration and by experience. Between these two shalts (pray and prove) are two shalt nots (quench not, depise not). The key is not just to ask God for help but to avoid closing down the sources of revelation, both those that come directly from the Spirit and those that come through "prophesyings," which I would understand to mean the inspired utterances of others.

The concluding phrase "hold fast the good" intrigued me. In my early morning revery, I had put a preposition in the last part of that passage, making it "hold fast *to* the good," as in "cling to the Iron Rod." As I read the entire epistle, particularly in the light of the Doctrine & Covenants, I began to think of the good we find in the Church somewhat differently. Even among Saints, virtues like love, forgiveness, and compassion are easily lost. In this sense, the good we find in the Church is less like a fixed pole, a safety railing on the break-down lane of life, than a living, breathing thing, sustained by our efforts. Like a toddler in a K-Mart, it can be gone in a minute if we blink. To "hold fast the good" is to protect and nurture Christian virtues in ourselves and in others. Within the Church, that is not only the best way, it is the only way. As Joseph Smith taught, "No power or influence can or ought to be maintained by virtue of the priesthood, only by persuasion, by long-suffering, by gentleness and meekness, and by love unfeigned" (D&C 121:41).

The fruits of the Spirit, as Paul tells us in Galatians, are "love, joy, peace, longsuffering, gentleness, goodness, faith, meekness, temperance" (5:22, 23). The opposites—hatred, variance, wrath, strife—come from the flesh. Since every human being is subject both to flesh and Spirit, we shouldn't be shocked when Latter-day Saints behave like other people. It is not just that fighting is wrong. It is inefficient, to use James Talmage's argument. As the Apostle Paul told the Galatians, when the Spirit and the flesh are in contention, "ye cannot do the things that ye would" (Gal. 5:17).

If the powers of heaven can only be exercised "upon principles of righteousness" (D&C 121:36), then unrighteous power is sham power. We make it real when we cower before it or when we answer it blow for blow. Lehi tells us that Christ's redemption leaves us free "to act" and "not to be acted upon" (2 Ne. 2:26). We lose our freedom when we let other people's behavior direct our energies. Paul puts it this way in Galatians:

> For all the law is fulfilled in one word, even in this; Thou shalt love thy neighbour as thyself.
> But if ye bite and devour one another, take heed that ye be not consumed one of another. (Gal. 5:14, 15)

Sometimes the best response to a would-be tyrant is to walk away quietly, leaving him with no one to oppress.

The ideal, of course, is to resolve the conflict lovingly. Paul urged the Thessalonians "to know them which labour among you, and are over you in the Lord, and admonish you" (5:12). Notice, he didn't say to obey them but to know them, and to "esteem them very highly in love for their work's sake" (5:13). He seemed less concerned about the issues that were dividing the Thessalonians than about the way they resolved those issues. He continued, "See that none render evil for evil unto any man, but ever follow that which is good, both among ourselves, and to all men" (5:15). He admonished them to "be at peace" (5:13) and he prayed that "the very God of peace" might sanctify them (5:13).

That advice is still good today. The kind of peace Paul envisioned can never be secured by decrees from Church headquarters, by press releases, or by demonstrations and manifestos from the ranks. It has to be built one-to-one, person-to-person, by "persuasion" and "long-suffering" and by "pure knowledge, which shall greatly enlarge the soul without hypocrisy, and without guile" (D&C 121:42). The Prophet wrote the long letter from which Doctrine and Covenants 121 and 122 are taken five months after the infamous "extermination order" that expelled the Saints from Missouri. He was still in prison, obviously angry at the mistreatment the Saints had received and dismayed at the behavior of men he had thought were his friends. The complete letter is longer, more personal, and in many ways less resolved than the passages that appear in the Doctrine & Covenants, but the ultimate focus, especially in those parts that became scripture, is not on oppression but on love. The prophet didn't tell the Saints how to reform their oppressors. Instead he taught them how to "wax strong in the presence of God" by giving up their own desire for dominion.

In warning us against the almost universal desire for unrighteous dominion, the Prophet taught us that true power must come "as the dews from heaven . . . without compulsory means" (D&C 121:45, 46). A righteous leader governs by "kindness, and pure knowledge . . . reproving betimes with sharpness when moved upon by the Holy Ghost." The last part of that passage is sometimes taken out of context, as though we can hurt and cut one another and then make it better by professing love. I cannot believe that the Holy Ghost moves people to anger and fear. Perhaps the "sharpness" envisioned is less a *wounding* sharpness than a *clarifying* sharpness.

220

In my experience, the most practical and little used method of resolving conflict is outlined in Doctrine & Covenants 42:88: "And if thy brother or sister offend thee, thou shalt take him or her between him or her and thee alone." The language is awkward; the meaning is unmistakable. If you have a problem with my behavior, tell me. Don't tell my bishop or my home teacher or the person next door. Give me a chance to repent or explain. Don't broadcast my sins from the mountain top or through Internet or hide them away in a secret file. Tell me in love. Do not reduce me to a label or a cartoon—a Raging Feminist, a Man in a Red Chair. Treat me as a brother or sister. "For God hath not appointed us to wrath, but to obtain salvation by our Lord Jesus Christ" (1 Thes. 5:9).

In the Sermon on the Mount, Jesus redefined the Mosaic law, substituting an ethic of mercy for a system of justice based on reciprocity. "Ye have heard that it hath been said, An eye for an eye, and a tooth for a tooth: But I say unto you, that ye resist not evil." Many Latter-day Saints would be grateful for mere justice, for social and ecclesiastical structures that truly returned love for love, service for service. Christ offers us more. Let us hold fast the good.

Note

[1] James E. Talmage, *Jesus the Christ*, 22nd edition, (Salt Lake City: Deseret Book Co., 1955), pp. 235–36.

Emma Lou Thayne • 1977

SPEAK OF REVERENCE FOR BEING

(Pound for Pound)

There must be a way
to retain the nobility of trees
and the surefootedness of rocks.

If we could sing always from here, canyon:
From here where the gold makes up to the green for staying,
Perhaps we could say what we must.

You would have to go with me
and never be idle, my canyon harmony.

Even to stagger about in the unholy city
and loiter in steamy meeting places.
You would have to stay like a cool flood of mountain water
companionable to difference.

In this crisp distance
pick up the scent, canyon.

Take yourself to the unsupposers,
to the lonely who have lost the presumption of dreams.
Unsettle their resignation.

Go to the talented and the willing
turned wan by the exploitation of the obvious.
Go as an orange wave from this mountain.

Carry your confounding to their oppressors
and tell of your refusal to give ear to them.

Slip into the mattresses of the wrongly mated
and issue your protest to those who give love by condescension.

Go among the guarded and diffident
or who have no love at all.

Go to the men and women swallowed by ungranted expectations.

Go to the wives cloistered in the complacency of arrival
and to the husbands gouged out
by the desolation of earning beyond spending
or spending beyond earning.

Go to the unmarried festering in being told
and tell of being.
Go against and for.

Rattle the cautious whose pores are calcified with formulas.

Give vision to the blind obeyers and to those who seek
something worth their obeying.

Go from here in exquisite candor.
Carry the harmony of leaves to sleeping and waking.

Take eager heed of new wrongs and new rights.

Go to the young who are laced by the bondage of pattern
and to those who have no pattern at all.
Sing of the relish of old and new.

Shout to those unacquainted with movement
whose blood and sweat have not been let free
by plunging and swinging audacious on waters or fields.

Whisper to those whose ages cannot be doubled,
whose lives are thickened by repetition.
Sharpen the memories of the informed who must now inform.

Tell them of the gold in the leaves
and the leaving that summons
the compounding of everything shaped or shaping.

Sing of the consummate gift of being used.

Go with the sureness of wondering
and the keenness of being in touch.

Take on the buoyance of birds.
Take root in the crevices of the world.

Hold to the rocks. Speak of reverence for being.
And be in favor of trees.

Dialogue by Fax:

PEGASUS

Salt Lake City, Utah
Saturday, 7 A.M.

Our dialogue is getting sort of heavy, maybe? Like being sick has been for me these past ten months. Don't you hate being sick? In months like this when some bug has taken up residence in me and turned my days indolent and wired with self-concern, I miss in my bones a chance to frolic. That's a word that was hard to explain to my Russian friend Valentina. Though she laughs often and richly, the deprivation of her childhood has precluded much indulgence in frolic. Right now she's visiting the country she loves, Russia, now in the throes of change even more frightening than when she left to come to teach at our university in America.

Thinking of those huge problems make mine seem minor. I'll get well. But, meantime, I miss my frolic. Like on the tennis court. I wrote a poem once about hitting a ball square, having the feeling ricochet up my arm and into my brain to send me reeling back and back and back to hit another ball.

But it's even more than that. It's doing it with the friends and family who love it too, the hitting, the running, the sweating and laughing—the frolic. Where else that giddy forgetting of everything beyond the moment? Hitting a golf ball right (rare) can be addictive for me or letting go on the ski hill or water skis or on the back of a horse playing Pegasus. But frolic? For me it's those crazy friends suspended for an hour and a half in what brings children giggling and squealing down a water slide or kids in heady contact on a soccer field. It's the privilege afforded by wellness and the freedom of testing a skill—no, of simply letting a skill have its way—and of forgetting everything else.

Sometimes I know that one hour of that kind of frolic could be more healing than any antibiotic or steroid or surgery or hospitalization or even sleep. What is your frolic, Laurel?

224

Durham, New Hampshire
Monday, 1:40 P.M.

My frolic is hitting ideas back to you. I never could play tennis, but I love a brisk game of words.

My sister-in-law used to joke that she didn't join the Thatcher family, she joined the Thatcher debating society. We used to have cookouts in Teton canyon in the summer just so we could sit around the picnic tables swatting horseflies and arguing about politics, or religion, or whether huckleberries tasted like blueberrries. As far as I know nobody in our family liked volleyball. Why get all sweaty when you could sit under a tree and talk?

I know. I am athletically disadvantaged. No doubt, I would be happier and healthier if I could water ski or winter ski or smack a ball with the flat of my hand, but in the aerobic department, I prefer walking. It is possible to walk and talk at the same time.

Some people have tennis pals or skiing buddies. I have talking partners, people who like nothing better than spending an hour on the telephone catching and throwing ideas, people who call me up at any hour of day or night to talk about important things (like recipes or war or this week's best movie they ever saw), people who haven't experienced something unless they've put it into words. Thanks for being one of those people. I would crumble in humiliation if you asked me to join you on a tennis court. But words! Let's go for it.

How about one last frolic? What on earth is Pegasus?

Salt Lake City, Utah
Tuesday, 2 P.M.

You remember—In Greek mythology, Pegasus is the winged horse sprung from Medusa at her death. With a blow of his hoof, he caused Hippocrene, the fountain of the Muses, to spring from Mount Helicon. Hence, poetic inspiration.

Any wonder that the winged horse has been my mount since girlhood in dreams and otherwise?

In the canyon sharing a bed with my grandma I used to go to sleep riding him off over the pines and into the sky where she told me he lived in a constellation named for him. Constellations I've only wondered about, but his inspiration has made a happy slave of me. To words and ideas and people. And like you, I'm glad. Just as I'm glad to have been one of your friends on the telephone wire, my writer friend Laurel. I send you and our readers that blessing of my canyon that still wings me off on the Pegasus journey I would wish for all of us—with love.

Durham, New Hampshire
Tuesday, 9 P.M.

Just a minute. You can't fly off yet until I explain my confusion about Pegasus. When I found him in the middle of your paragraph about golf balls and soccer, I thought you were alluding to a game played on horseback, like polo. That's the historian in me. I keep my magnifying glass close to the ground. I should have known how poetry hovers behind every word you write, how easily you lift into the sky. I'm glad I made it as far as the telephone wire and caught you in landing.

Medusa? Isn't she the woman with snakes in her hair? The angry one? The scary one? The gorgon who frightened men into stone? I am delighted to know that in her own way she gave birth to poetry. Thanks to you I am delighted about a whole lot else as well. This morning I looked up from my computer, a year after this project began, to see the maple outside my window ignite against blue sky.

Thanks for bringing me home to our common branch.

Salt Lake City, Utah
Wednesday, noon

Isn't this typical, Laurel, that in finding all these ways we're alike, there are still differences that we can work out by coming together to talk—on the page or singing out loud in the choir. Thank you for teaching and learning with me, my friend. I'm ready for the snow to fall, my seasons seasoned by where we've been and where I'm sure we've yet to go.

TRAVELING

It's about borders.
Out there the land screams at its edges;
that is, people think it should.
So they send armies to shrink or bloat
what map makers have drawn
from the yankings of history.

On the borders they expect right
to stay on one side. But it thumps
and howls, skinning the sky
that never stops. It is borders
that suggest, give permission,
invite the yours and the mine
of the quarrels, separate, kill.

A border would divide even a piece of time
into here and hereafter.

But what a traveler finds
is that no one administrates
what flows between people.
Mortal connectedness, as if from enormous wings,
orders the comings, their passages,
the dissolution of borders in light
and the breath of human exchange.

Funny it took taking to the sky, then space
to obscure the detail, to let the traveler know
no matter how real, the borders don't exist:
They're only thinly dotted lines,
like the traveler, herself a small bundle of fibers
poised for passing when the soul
eradicates borders
and anywhere you go is going home.

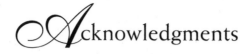

Acknowledgments

We would like to thank the Women's Research Center at Brigham Young University for initiating this project; Dawn Hall Anderson, who made the original selections, nurtured new work, and offered guidance along the way; the many readers, some of them anonymous, who reviewed the manuscript; Darla Isackson and Giles Florence and their staff at Aspen Books for skillful editing; Amy Ulrich, who at an early stage offered thoughtful comments on our essays; and the editors of the publications where our essays first appeared, particularly Susan Paxman of *Exponent II*. Finally, we thank our husbands, Gael and Mel, who unfailingly support us on our common branch.

We would like to thank the editors of the following essays for use in whole or part of pieces that originally appeared in their publications:

"Abigail," *Exponent II*, Spring 1991.
"Applause," *Exponent II*, Summer 1986.
"Border Crossings," *Dialogue*, vol. 27, Summer 1994.
"Chiaroscuro," *Exponent II*, Spring 1982.
"Danish Pancakes," *Exponent II*, Fall 1985.
"First Loss," *Until Another Day for Butterflies* (Salt Lake City: Parliament Publishers), 1973.
"Good-bye, Virginia Slims," *Exponent II*, Spring 1984.
"Grace Under Pressure," *Exponent II*, Winter 1987.
"A History Lesson," *Exponent II*, Spring 1985.
"I Am Delighted," *Things Happen: Poems of Survival* (Salt Lake City: Signature Books), 1991.
"Improve the Shining Moments," *Exponent II*, Spring 1994.
"Landscapes of the Mind," *Exponent II*, Spring 1989; *network* magazine, April 1989.
"A Little Bit of Heaven," *Dialogue*, vol. 9, Fall 1975.
"Lusterware," *A Thoughtful Faith*, ed. Philip L. Barlow (Centerville, Utah: Canon Press), 1986.

"Milk and Honey Motherhood," *Exponent II*, Spring 1984.

"Models and Heroes," *Exponent II*, Winter 1986.

"Neighbors," *Ensign*, June 1988.

"Night Light," *Exponent II*, Winter 1985.

"Ode to Autumn," *Exponent II*, Fall 1981.

"On the Side of Life," published in its original form by *network*, magazine, January 1986, and *Exponent II*, Fall 1990.

"Patchwork," *Exponent II*, Spring, 1988.

"A Phi Beta Kappa Key and a Safety Pin," *Exponent II*, Spring 1992.

"A Pioneer Is Not a Woman Who Makes Her Own Soap," *Ensign*, June 1978.

"Poor Mother," *Dialogue*, vol. 10, Spring 1975/6.

"Rip Off," *On Slim, Unaccountable Bones* (Salt Lake City: Parliament Publishers), 1974.

"Resist Not Evil," *Exponent II*, Fall 1994.

"Speak of Reverence for Being," *A Woman's Place* (Salt Lake City: Nishan Grey, Inc.), 1977.

"Time for the Inner Music," *Exponent II*, Winter 1984.

"Valentina," published in its original form by *network* magazine, May 1988, and *Desert Sun*, Spring 1988.

"Visiting Teaching," *Exponent II*, Summer 1983, Winter 1984. (Printed under the name of "A Morsel Of Bread" and "Myrtle" in this volume.)

"What Time Is It?" published in its original form by *BYU Studies*, October 1986.

"With Love, Mother," published in its original form by the *Ensign*, May 1973, and subsequently as a booklet (Salt Lake City: Deseret Book Co.), 1975.

"A Word from the Whys: Listening to My Teenager," *Ensign*, March 1980.

"You Tell Me Your Dreams and I'll Tell You Mine," published in its original form by *Exponent II*, Winter 1993. A later version was prepared for presentation at a Women's Conference at BYU and then published in *Women in the Covenant of Grace* (Salt Lake City: Deseret Book Co.), 1994.